I AM STARSEED

An Angelic Starseed Awakening Story

Activating the Starseed Mission on Earth

Xi EarthStar Healer

www.earthstar.tk

ISBN - 9798618274340

Cover Painting by Bástian Roa

https://www.facebook.com/roa.bastian.art/

DNA Helix Art by Margherita Gramiccia

I dedicate this Work to the Bad-Ass Shining Millennial Starseeds

*Who will pave the way for the Rainbow-Crystal
Children of our Future*

& the First Wave Indigos who Paved the Way for Me to Shine.

Thank you for your Service & Love of All of Creation.

May you Forever be Blessed in the Heavens, of All that Is

Table of Contents

Introduction vii

Chapter 1: The Early Years 1

Chapter 2: The Call of Creation: A Bachelor's Degree of Magic
in the University of Life 4

Chapter 3: Dreams of Galactivation 14

Chapter 4: Shamanic Initiation 32

Chapter 5: Defense Against the Dark Arts 44

Chapter 6: False Matrix Correction 60

Chapter 7: Pleiadian Goddess Vortex 68

Chapter 8: Sasquatch Rescue 75

Chapter 9: Stargate SG-1 & the Astral Military 84

Chapter 10: Titicaca, Tiwanaku & Ancient Creation Magic 95

Chapter 11.: Ariana: Sexual Misery Programming 107

Chapter 12. Beyond Amnesia: Portals to the New Earth 120

Chapter 13: The Starseed Mission & the Stages of
    Starseed Awakening..133

    Earthstar Healers 133

    Am I a Starseed? 139

    The Different Waves of the Starseed Mission 142

    Higher Self Embodiment as a Walk-In Process 148

    The Stages of Starseed Awakening 154

    Channels to Embodied Masters 168

    Coming into Wholeness 169

    Lucidity Medicine for the Great Sickness 174

    Angelic Consciousness 176

Introduction

My name is Xi EarthStar Healer, and this is my story of Awakening on Planet Earth as an Angelic Starseed. Embedded within this transmission are Light Codes of Source Consciousness which are triggers for Starseed Activation. I am but One of Hundreds of Thousands of Starseeds Incarnate on Earth now.

At this time in my Embodiment process I am accessing and integrating into my Body my Higher Dimensional Selves, recovering the knowledge and experiences I gained in lifetimes spent in various places on Earth as well as other locales in the Universe such as Andromeda, Pleiades and Sirius in preparation for this present Lifetime.

For example, the predominant skills and aspect of Self which facilitates my genetic / shamanic healing work is my 7D Andromedan aspect, who is a light-field geneticist. In lifetimes studying genetics in a higher dimension I learned how to maneuver, create and alter genetic coding from a higher perspective via consciousness, a skill which I am pulling into my physical body now.

Through these years of Activation, I no longer have any fear or doubt surrounding the Truth of being a Starseed. From this state of integration, I share with you the stories of my awakening and journey into Truth, Love and Beauty of our existence.

These journeys are how I came to discover for myself the darkness which plagued the Earth: the negative astral influencers, DNA degradation, artificial reality, and its effects on Humanity. They also allowed me to discover my own soul's antidotes to the Great Sickness of Separation. I feel that the sharing of these stories make for an excellent way to share what I as a galactic anthropologist have learned about our starseeded nature, and our collective mission here on Earth.

My Heart's desire is that through sharing stories of my own healing, others will find clues to their own, and through my Activation experiences, others will begin to deeply acknowledge their own innate connection to Nature, our Starseed beingness, and align deeper into a Life of Divine Purpose.

My awakening journey was the access point into higher-sense awareness and multidimensional lightwork. Participation and devotion to the Mystery School of my Life initiated me and showed me all that was necessary to activate my Self as a Custodian and Guardian of the New Earth. In this context, these stories of my awakening set the stage for my next book: Advanced Lightwork: Medicine for the Great Sickness - A Guided Process of Self Healing, Activation & Initiation into Multi-Dimensional Energy Work.

I also hope that through the sharing of my story, Starseeds can reconcile with their Parents, who maybe have had a hard time connecting with or understanding their millennial Starseed children.

It is my Prayer that All Remember the Awe, Wisdom and Magic within Each and every One of us, and that we wield the Magic of Source Creation in Strength and Empowerment for the Liberation of All Beings.

~ ❈ ~

CHAPTER 1

The Early Years

I was born in North-East China in a province called LiaoNing in 1994, when the Earth, Sun and Sirius star system were in perfect heliocentric alignment.

The Earth had just entered the Photon belt and a new wave of Light Energies were radiating onto the planet. Despite my father's adamant disbelief in all things supernatural, he read an astrology based child-naming book for 3 days before choosing a name for me. According to the Stars, my birth name for this incarnation was to be XiangMing ~ roughly translated to mean Fragrant Medicinal Tea.

I had an average, middle class, atheist and religiously neutral family, yet I remember writing Taoist poetry about the eternal changing nature of Time and seeing visions of the "false matrix" when I was 5 years old. I always felt like I was in connection with something mysteriously wonderful, like there were bubbles of Magic all around me.

When I was 9, my family moved from a small industrial town in China to Ontario, Canada. I attended public school and learned English, and as modern society molded me to fit inside of it, the spark inside me dwindled. My ESL teacher gave me a new name, "Shawna", an earth persona I lived out for the following 8 years. It always felt like a part of me was missing then. Over time this developed into severe depression, suicidal thoughts and a severe eating disorder that almost took my life in my late teens.

In my high school years I lived a double life. Inside one frame, I was fighting with a mental discontent which controlled my life. My parents were culturally Chinese, and they raised me that way. Everyone in my school was Caucasian, and I nonchalantly wanted to be a part of it. Even still, I quickly discovered in the first months of high school that Gossip Girls and lip gloss was not at all appealing to me - I slipped through the halls of High School dancing with the fairies in my imagination.

Unbeknownst to me at the time, the Dark had mapped my coordinates for my arrival on Earth and tagged me as a danger to their dank operations. Since the moment I was born, they influenced my energy field and unsuspecting parents in ways which intended to destroy my Light.

These multidimensional astral disturbances compounded by the spiritual unrest of colonized native land my subdivision was built on top of eventually lead to my severe anorexia, bulimia and depression mid-way through high school.

In my shamanic work now I am discovering that this is a common occurrence for Starseeds. We usually choose to enter the planet during specific stellar alignments. Like a shooting star, we are a streak of bright light piercing through the polluted astral plane. Because of this, it was easy for astral beings to know when and where we are coming in.

We knew this before we came, and it did not deter our will to be here.

Beyond all interference, I arrived safely in my Body with all my codons in tact. And every interaction with the Dark and their silly tactics have only taught me more about their tricks. Early training in Defence against the Dark Arts.

I understand now that as a Starseed, the process of getting lost in the Dark was an essential part of my Training. To experience the grief of losing our creativity and magic, very much like all of humanity did, gifted me with a deep sense of compassion and infinite motivation to find the Cure.

CHAPTER 2

The Call of Creation: A Bachelor's Degree of Magic in the University of Life

In the fall of 2012 I was 18. I knew I had to get away from Ontario and the controlling grip of my parents so I decided to pursue a degree in classical piano in Montreal. After spending only 3 months in university, it became blatantly clear that that was not my scene.

In February of 2013, I followed my heart and quit piano school. I had no idea what I was doing. And as the icing on the cake, I lost my home and nearly all of my belongings in the matter of a couple of weeks. This was the proverbial moment when my whole life turned upside down, and I was out on the cold barren streets with literally nothing.

Walking down the snowy streets of Montreal in February one night with only $10 left in my pocket, I murmured to the invisible: there must be something You are leading me towards... why else would this be happening to me? I remember this moment like a lucid postcard in my mind because it was very strange to me.

My parents were atheists and I had no prior understanding of mysticism in this life. Yet as if this inner knowing took over my mind, somehow I just knew I was in communication with the force of Life. As I prayed, I walked past a Chinese buffet. Mind you it was 11 PM, so I thought it was very strange to hear a steady "boom boom boom boom!" coming out of the large barred doors.

You have to know that up until this very moment, I have been a studious and quiet Chinese girl all of my life. I had never heard of electronic music nor knew that people danced to it all night sometimes. It was very cold, and I figured, where else could I go? I braved the Rave and entered the booming buffet. I handed the doorman my only $10 and was given a rite of passage.

The story continues into the night; I befriended a crew of electronic music party organizers and DJs named "Third Eye crew". They mostly spoke French but some special intrigue surrounded our encounter and they took me in as one of their own.

I'd never been exposed to partying nor electronic music before, nor chakras nor psychedelics. I had no idea what a third eye was. And if I was being perfectly honest, I didn't even really know what having a friend felt like. Yet somehow beyond all that, they trusted me and I trusted them. They offered for me to stay with them for the winter months. From them I took my first lessons in ethics and philosophies of Rave culture, and what it is to Awaken and to be on a Mission to Awaken others.

~ ✤ ~

In March of 2013, whilst sitting in the back of a taxi I spontaneously asked myself: "Where Am I From?" Firstly, I was intrigued that I would ask myself such a question; secondly, I assumed of course that my mind would simply reply "China." To my own bewilderment, the immediate answer which resounded back to me was "Andromeda."

The first thing I did when I got home was google "beings from Andromeda" ~ this is how I came to find a vast array of information about Starseeds on the internet. Over the next months and years, I began to consciously commune and communicate with Higher Dimensional beings of Consciousness and Light. I realized that it was their guidance, presence, and support that had always been around me. I also realized that they are often higher dimensional aspects of my Self.

There is One Force of Consciousness all around and within us, and something happens when we begin to communicate with this Force. Even that which seem like simple mundanity to us have consciousness, and everything is Alive. This is probably the most incredible thing I could report to anyone at this point in my journey. The fabric of reality is Consciousness, and it is always interacting with us whether we are aware of it or not.

On the surface level we experience repeating synchronous number sequences, the tip of the iceberg. If really begin to pay attention, and deeply commit to listening and responding to the world based on our inner feelings - we are lead into re-alignment with our organic soul timelines. My first initiation into this re-alignment was becoming homeless yet through following my connection to the Invisible, becoming adopted by this Third Eye family of Awakeners.

As time went by in my new life, I began to feel something eerily off with the reality I was living in. Cement, junk food, television ~ none of it was arousing to Life. None of it felt very good. Nobody looked like they enjoyed it, even when they pretended to.

We the raving youth were frustrated with the way society was. We didn't have enough money to live, and if we wanted to have money we would have to conform to a version of ourselves which wasn't true to our hearts and sell our precious time.

The psychedelic children remained loving and accepting of All in the world. We created a bubble of our own amusement, a wild and mystical space which allowed us to explore and come into our Selves.

In the late spring of 2013, I enjoyed countless nights dancing amongst happy and magical people dressed in colourful costumes, feeling accepted and celebrated for all of our uniqueness, having authentic and heartfelt interactions with strangers. In the day I scoured for money at my day job as a telemarketer, awarded to manipulate and lie to other human beings to get their money for a truly useless service. The polarity between these two realities tore my soul a part, and brought me in touch with an agony which pierced through my heart and soul.

The dichotomy of the different worlds I walked and the unarguable presence of a tension in the citizens of the artificial world was driving me into this dense knot in my belly. For many years I tried to numb this insurmountable pain through addictive and sabotaging behaviors and pretended it wasn't there. But now I couldn't bare to deny it any longer. I screamed out to the Invisible.

I found myself in a state of hopelessness and despair. And as if my body knew me better than I consciously knew myself at the time, I walked out into the forest.

I fell to the ground in tears, and in complete surrender and release, I uttered: "Earth, Sky, if you can hear me, I must let you know that I am very distraught. I can feel your grace and love for me through all that the Invisible has provided me. Yet I must know what I can do for Humanity and the Earth. You, Earth and Sky, know the World and Me better than myself, so you must know better than I how I can best be of service! Call on me and provide for me and I will be there! I pledge my allegiance to the Creation of Heaven on Earth for All!"

Well, my prayer worked. Soon after this dramatic universal profession, I began to hear the whispers of Mama Gaia through the wind and trees and my star family telling me where to go and how to get there. When I entrusted and completely surrendered my Life and Curiosity to their gentle nudges of guidance, I found myself living inside an indescribably magical Reality.

In that moment of complete surrender, my knees and hands felt the support of the Earth and wind as it caressed my skin and spirit. I saw an enormous rift between my personal experience of the Aliveness of the Universe, the love I felt for All of Creation, and the depth and understanding of reality most people had. Deep within me roared a sense of having a deeper purpose. I felt lost in how to discover it.

~ ✼ ~

For the majority of 2013 and 2014 I attended many Conscious Music festivals and conscious dance parties. A deep part of my psyche was always making notes and discovering the undercurrents of these events. On the surface it looked to be a bunch of people dancing. On a planetary and galactic level, the energies of joy and unity that built up from these events acted like Planetary acupuncture, radiating love and excitement out onto the planet.

A part of me was always researching. I'd start to speak to others about what I was noticing and often received blank stares. I was tapping into a field of knowing where higher dimensional light technologies of awakening and activation were in play, but not many others were aware of this.

I experienced many shamanic initiations during this period of my life, activating psychic capabilities most are not aware of. It was felt and known that my intimate relationship with the Invisible force was training and preparing me for something bigger. This relationship with a grander aspect of me nourished me and filled up my void with trust and comfort.

I first awakened to my psychic healing powers viscerally manipulating energy and consciousness on the dance floor. My guides always informed me that this was only the beginning of my shamanic training - a strangely competent place for this sort of exploration.

One time around 2 AM, I left the party tired from dancing and went to Arby's for a late night rootbeer float. Surprised to find 10 people in line before me, in my ecstatic state I decided to play a game. I asked the person in front of me if they'd play rock, paper, scissors with me - and if I won I'd get to go ahead of them in line. Practicing my psychic abilities, I'd project the losing choice into their mind, play the winning hand and move ahead in line. I played this game until I was at the front of the line, having won 8 games of rock paper scissors in a row.

This was the beginning of my active training in psionic redaction, which is a capability I now use to heal collective, planetary and galactic grid-lines of energy and consciousness. I also use this ability to project into another's body or consciousness to facilitate psychic surgery, soul retrieval, and light body and consciousness repair.

I enjoyed thinking that I was attending my own magic university, and I decided that the next few years would be my Bachelor's degree.

I asked the universe to throw me a graduation party, with my favorite DJs, with epic magic people, when my studies are complete in this phase of my life. I enjoyed this whimsical thought often and smiled at the possibility.

One of the key things I learned about the festival world was that it was a playground for awakened beings to explore and discover possible templates for society. A society based on imagination, love, creativity and play! What would we do if we were on a Heavenly planet with Friends of all shapes and colors?

~ ❀ ~

By this time I was regularly tapping into a different state of being, in which my body feels more coherent, fluid and light, my heart feels more open and content and my mind feels one with the Infinite. In these spaces I would communicate with my Star family, receiving assurance, healing, and guidance.

When I felt down or frustrated, my body was led to walk outside and my head would spontaneously tilt to the sky as if someone was moving my body for me. When my eyes hit the stars, an instant flush of relief, unconditional love and support would flow through me. Sometimes I would start to weep at the amount of Love and Understanding I felt from them.

I started to trust and integrate the fact that there are interdimensional beings who are family to me, who were by my side.

Towards the end of 2013, I took some misfortuned magic pills from a stranger at a psytrance party and had my first contact and near death experience. Looking back this was a planned excursion to accelerate my true galactic higher self's walk-in process.

I actually went up to this man since I'd seen him give these pills to other people. I was very adventurous and naive at this time, and thought it would be fun to experience the rave in an altered state. Since parties and gatherings like this always ended up becoming shamanic training for me, I figured this would be another fun night of moving energy and aligning energy fields.

An hour or two after ingesting the pills, I started to feel really funny. The familiar loving swirls of light and sound were greatly exaggerated and an environment of chaos and discombobulation started to overtake my consciousness. Something was wrong. It took me a few more minutes to realize that my body was having an adverse reaction to this mysterious pill and I might actually be overdosing.

In my swirling psychedelic haze I made my way to the bathroom. Once I arrived inside the stall, my eyes could no longer see anything but a giant pink glaze, the bathroom stall no longer existed and I was floating inside a pink vortex. I started to throw up violently and felt my consciousness begin to fade. The thought and fear of death did cross my mind, but I also felt like a significant moment in my life was occurring simultaneously.

As these thoughts slid through my mind like silly putty on a hot day, a small ET saucer appeared and was rapidly flying towards me out of the pink vortexing portal. As soon as it got close enough for me to see that there were two beings inside, a red laser shot out from the ship. It zapped me once in each eye and then manipulated the space around me to align my spine, and it literally walked my limp body back into the party onto a couch where some of my friends were sitting.

I guess then I passed out because the next moment I remember, I was coming back into presence. I was back inside the environment of the party - the pink swirls were gone - and my friends were sitting around me on this couch having a jolly conversation.

"How long was I asleep for?" I asked, as I yawned, stretched and sat up.

"Mmm, probably like 30 minutes? Pretty early to be taking naps at the party don't you think?", they mocked. I'm usually the one on the dancefloor playing with energy right into the morning; I guess it was odd for me to be asleep at the rave.

I decided to get up and give dancing a try. The next moments in time surprised me to no end. My body and consciousness felt so coherent, fluid and alive, like I'd been doing hours of yoga and breathwork. My body was the healthiest and consciousness the brightest I've ever felt in my whole entire life!

I remembered everything that happened with the ETs, and it didn't feel abnormal or strange at all. It felt regular, like I just ate a sandwich for lunch, as if some part of me always knew that was a part of my plan. It allowed the opportunity for what I now know as a Pleiadian beamer ship to interfere and totally re-align my body-spirit connection so more of my higher self can exist inside my body.

My earth self learned something that day. This event jumped my entire being onto a higher timeline: Activating my Starseed mission. Any part of my 3D self that still had any doubt about my purpose on Earth vanished. Lots of people die from overdosing all the time. These interdimensional beings knew me and came to support me for a reason.

Life became different and flowed more quickly after that. A fluid ecstatic light flowed around me, and I often found myself in a totally different state of consciousness than others around me. While people continued on their mundane false matrix activities, going to their day jobs and having boring conversations with each other about nothing, I watched and stayed silent in deep observation…

Something deep, deep inside me was changing, and this will probably lead to an enormous external reality shift. Knowing I had little to do with the planning of my bachelor's degree of magic, I surrendered to the love of the Divine and rested assured in the path that laid brightly ahead for me.

CHAPTER 3

Dreams of Galactivation

The harsh winter of early 2015 was just coming to an end. After spending 2 years interwoven into the psychedelic scenery of raves and festivals, I finally received directions from the wind.

Walking down the street one rainy spring afternoon, I had an overwhelming inclination to close my eyes. I stood still. In awe and surprise, a beautiful, colorful vision began to formulate in my mind's eye!

In this vision I saw a large building that vaguely resembled the shape of a hospital or university. Lush plants grew all around and from inside and on top of it. Very happy people were coming in and out.

I could see the inside of the building too, where many were taking various classes on galactic history, multidimensionality, consciousness, perma-culture, sustainability… All aspects of a well-rounded, conscious Civilization were represented! Children ran and played in the flowering gardens of abundance and beauty.

In the vision I could see around the peripherals that this was a template holistic healing and creative living education center designed to assist the mass populace in healing from planetary enslavement and remembering humanity's true purpose and place in the universe as divine creator beings! These centres are going to be built in all major cities around the world. When I returned to my body, I knew this was a part of my Purpose.

Some days after receiving this vision, I was sitting around at home thinking about tobacco use. I had been an avid smoker since 10th grade, and I needed more empirical research on the negative effects of its extended use to help me curb the habit. Into Google I entered "lower vibration cigarettes."

To my intrigue the fifth link immediately caught my eye - it read "5th Dimensional Community." I followed the link onto a plain text page outlining a community project in Zuni Mountains, New Mexico. Picturesque memories of the vision returned to my mind.

Without much thought as if my body was running itself, I wrote a simple email to the admin of the page: "Are you a group of fully-activated human beings? How many are you? How many acres have you got?"

Within 3 hours I received a full length report of the vision of the project, details eerily close to the visions I had, from a man named Rich. I began to jitter in excitement as waves of relief washed over my entire being finally receiving confirmation that these multidimensional states and experiences were not due to a malfunctioning brain!

Rich and I chatted on the phone for a few hours and continued to converse over the internet. We were filled with a soul-level familiarity. My consciousness and body shifted in ways difficult to explain in words. It brought me an incredible sense of agility, love, lucidity and excitement. I understand these feelings now as sensations of Activation & Spirit Incarnation.

It didn't require much thinking on my part as the signs were plenty clear that this manifestation was directly related to the vision. The synchronicity was difficult to deny. At some point Rich mentioned that this land was actually purchased by a now deceased man, who always said he was from Andromeda. I never told Rich that my first Starseed awakening experience was finding out I was from Andromeda! I booked a flight to New Mexico.

The magic that ensued from this adventure and its unfolding still leaves me in Awe, even after all these years.

~ ✲ ~

It started off at Vipassana, synchronously 12 days before my plane ticket was booked to New Mexico, over the Lunar Eclipse of March 2015. Before this point I'd never practiced much meditation. Remember that deeply ingrained skepticism of all societal institutions? Well if it was present for the education system, you bet it was even stronger applied to schools of spirituality. I thought, if people can just think about world peace while sitting on their buns, why hasn't it manifested already?

I thought, if there was a pothole in the middle of the street and one person thinks it should be fixed, she could sit and meditate on the pot-hole being fixed. And even if this worked, then she could really just be spiritually influencing someone else to do the hard work of actually fixing the pot-hole. Then my bad-ass millennial starseed self would think: "Alright, so people meditated for aliens to come, so here we are… Here I Am."

Just as a side note, I do realize that sometimes my "bad-ass millennial starseed self" can come off as seeming a little narcissistic or arrogant, but I think this is a part of my starseed genes too. I imagine if I didn't have this personality trait, I'd probably get distracted by all that shines and glitters in the new age spirituality cults or get squashed by the false matrix. This starseed gene expression was purposely coded for the protection of my inner knowing.

I knew I was guided to be at Vipassana at this time, so I was looking forward to my experience. For anyone who may not know, Vipassana is a great place to go for a meditation retreat. It is a donation based 10 day silent meditation retreat which provides food and lodging. There are centres all over the world.

My resistant disposition towards meditation quickly dispersed as my experience there deepened; I realized I was in for a treat! From the moment I sat down to meditate, I could feel the presence of my Galactic team all around me.

For the first 3 days, I was guided to do a meditation similar to that which was being taught but in a more expedited fashion. I felt bad about deviating from the taught curriculum of the meditation centre, but the calling to practice what was guided was so strong. Still just as the course was guiding us, I released blocked energies that manifested as tension while traumatic memories surfaced and washed away, surfaced and washed away...

My psychic senses opened up and I was able to feel what I perceived to be blockages and implants in my body. This was my first visceral experience of interdimensional implantation and this has expanded into a huge part of my work now as a light and energy worker.

The first implant I perceived was a 3-pronged metal feeling object lodged in my cervix. It created tension and a great deal of sadness, and as I meditated I saw it dissolve into a mesh of light that my meditation powered. As this blockage dissolved, energy trickled down my legs and places in my body shivered and popped. My energy field as well as my conscious awareness lit up and expanded. For 3 days this went on, as blockages and implants from other parts of my body were worked on and removed.

The shifts in my consciousness this sort of energy body clearing provided was palpable. As distortions in the geometry of my multidimensional body were restored to their original perfection, waves of peace, love, acceptance, patience, presence and creativity poured through my consciousness and body. Some would refer to these ecstatic states as bliss. I prefer to use the term peace. Our natural state of being.

Feeling the incredible shifts in my awareness, feeling more 'myself' and 'home' in my own body than I ever have, I experienced a deep realization that all of humanity had been duped. Duped into believing we are anything less than sovereign and duped into believing we have to work hard to be accepted or loved by God and each other. We were duped into believing that we aren't inherently spiritual and perfect!

Cultural collective belief systems leave billions of people in a state of desolation, fear, purposelessness, meaninglessness, lifelessness... yet this couldn't be further from the Truth!

Piercing through the layers of programming, implants, and distortions in my consciousness and energy body gave me a clear look at the reality. This clarity and ability to see the infinite dimensions of the construct of reality continues to unfold and expand in my work as a multidimensional field repair technician, aka grid worker.

Taoist philosophers speak of becoming aware of the conditioned mind and returning to the awakened mind. I realized that culture heavily influenced what individuals residing within that cultural umbrella deemed as normal. A mind molded and constructed by its environment is this conditioned mind.

After 3 days of focusing my energy on pacifying excess or unbalanced energies in my body I was entirely free of negative thoughts. My baseline awareness of my own consciousness was feelings of peace, joy, curiosity and compassion. I knew the Truth, that this is Human Nature. The Nature of the biological consciousness expression known as Human is Love.

For the second 3 days information and visions began flowing freely to my mind during meditation about New Earth Healing Centres, a new healing modality of my own, and reconfigured ways to achieve psycho-physical healing. For awhile I identified this seemingly other stream of thoughts within my mind as an Alien ~ now I know it is my Higher Selves & my Star collective consciousness.

During days 4 to 6, another very curious experience was had. A being appeared on a cloud, I felt him as Buddha, he told me he was sort of like my star uncle yet in another sense my nephew. In his presence I felt a great peace and contentment in my heart space. With an amicable smirk he told me that the videos and teachings at the retreat centre were out-dated and began to make corrections to the discourse as it went on.

He told me that these teachings were designed for a people who lived in an entirely different culture and state of civilization and consciousness evolution, over thousands of years ago. At that time, enlightenment simply required achievement of liberation by the individual being. However now enlightenment is a collective movement and requires a whole humanity to express its fullness.

Although the majority of the core principles remain (like Love and Unity), many practices and schools are in need of major renovation to truly be applicable and helpful in the modern world.

I was bewildered. Of course I had known this intuitively, you know, my bad-ass millennial starseed codes. But I did not expect Buddha himself to come and tell me these things. He continued to show me visions of modern practices and teachings I am still unpacking to this day, which make up the foundation of Advanced Lightwork.

After meditating 8-10 hours a day for an entire 8 days, my senses and mental clarity were greatly heightened. I felt light as a feather, and a brilliant joy was emanating from my heart. I was dancing down the hallways humming, in a mood I can only imagine fairies are in all the time living in enchanted forests.

Knowing I only had a couple of days between the retreat and my flight out to New Mexico, I quietly hoped I could somehow get out of the retreat a couple days sooner. I was also enthralled by my inter-dimensional experiences and realizations and wondered if private discourses with Buddha on the inner planes of consciousness happen to everyone at Vipassana.

I signed up for a private question session with the meditation teacher on the morning of the 8th day. I explained to her what had been happening during my retreat so far. To my surprise her complexion turned white and she hastily said in nervousness, "come back in 30 minutes."

When I returned to her office after 30 minutes, she informed me that I would have to leave the meditation centre immediately on the pretense that apparently a staff member had seen me talking to another retreat participant. This is an illegal act inside the retreat. Though most times when you are caught doing this, you get a warning, not immediate expulsion!

Confused, I retorted that I'd really like to continue the retreat and that I was sorry to bring up these uncomfortable questions… She was very adamant that I had to leave. The retreat was 2 hours outside of Montreal in a very small town, pretty much in the middle of nowhere. My friends were unable to pick me up at that moment.

When I returned to my room to collect my items, I found all my belongings packed up already. A staff member ushered me and my things into a car, and insisted that I call again from a pay phone in town. When I explained to her I didn't have any money on me, she didn't seem to care at all, and upon arriving in town she hastily evicted me from her car and drove off.

I gathered myself in an empty parking lot looking around in this eerie ghost town. There was literally no one around and none of the businesses were even in operation. The pay phone was broken. I decided the only reasonable thing to do at this point was to walk towards the highway.

I thought, 'I could hitch a ride back to Montreal'. As soon as my feet brought me onto the highway, without even sticking out my thumb, a truck stopped beside me. The driver rolled down his window and invited me in.

Plunged back out into the "real world" again after 8 full days of meditation was a real riot! The world swirled in brilliant colours, similar to being on a mild dose of some psychedelic. A couple days later, a friend of mine who was at the same Vipassana retreat contacted me via social media to tell me that on the 8th night of the retreat, she dreamt I was being rescued from the building and on the morning of the 9th day I disappeared.

I would be leaving in 3 days to New Mexico for my adventure, and the positive effects of the intensive meditation had me feeling like my brain was a Quartz crystal all 3 days.

~ ❀ ~

Ever have that feeling in your gut and Spirit that there is something you have to do, or a part of you that seeks reconciliation, yet to everyone else you sound Crazy? I still feel that way sometimes, but the intensity of my Inner Gnosis is so strong, to deny it would be a crime of betrayal to my own soul.

When I told my roommates and friends in Montreal about my decisions to go to New Mexico, they were dumbfounded. It wasn't just that I was going on a trip, but that I made the decision to immediately go on the trip based on a hallucination and a random person I found on the Internet, which I am decidedly calling Synchronicity. The morning before my flight, 10 of my friends showed up at my house while I was packing, in an attempted intervention to convince me not to go.

"You might die. You don't even know this person, and you're going to hang out with him in the forest by yourself on a one-way plane ticket? Do you know what you're doing there?"

They ambushed me with questions and fears, doubts and concerns which I had already gone through at least 100 times in my own head. But the more they yammered, the more I was certain I was doing the right thing.

I didn't understand vibrational resonance yet, but I recognized that I felt really good when I thought or talked about interdimensional ETs, New Earth and Healing Centres… A feeling I couldn't really explain to any of them, so I just smiled and said: "I have to do this. It's that simple for me."

Through all their chattering I managed to pack up my suit-case, and as I rolled out unto the open pavement I had never felt so Free in my entire life. I was excited for a very purposeful journey, and the openness of endless possibility smelled like a gentle gust of cool spring air.

A significant shift in the Field of Reality was sensed as soon as I left the bubble of other people and returned to my own body and awareness. A feeling that every molecule of everything is conscious and One and in constant loving support and communication with me.

I had a 12 hour lay-over in Chicago, and I was very sleepy and tired from all the excitement. In innocence I telepathically asked the Airport for a blanket and a place to sleep. Immediately my body responded to an energy wave which guided my body to a specific place in the airport where a new blanket inside a plastic package sat on a chair with no one else around! It beckoned me. Half shocked and half having anticipated this, I thanked the spirit of the airport, my angels, grabbed the blanket and fell asleep behind a billboard.

~ ✿ ~

When I arrived in New Mexico, I was picked up by my new friend Rich. The sky was as open as I'd ever experienced it, the air was warm and fresh, and I felt only the excitement of a brand new adventure. We picked up some groceries and headed to the Land which called me. I stayed there in the forest for about 2 weeks. Ever present was the feeling of my skull opening up and my crown becoming one with the cosmic sky.

I now understand this process as connecting and merging my crown and light body to the central sun, the collective consciousness and the field of oneness of all that is. This is what I refer to as Galactivation. Activating our Galactic Consciousness. The inner sky scintillating with consciousness and living light, expanding into infinity, is a physical sensation of Galactivation, coupled with heightened feelings of connection with the Aliveness which flows through all things.

As our consciousness expands onto the galactic level, understanding the flow of life force and its constrictions on planet earth becomes evident. One puts the pieces together and accesses truth directly from the present moment.

Living on the Land was free and simple. Each morning we meditated, then ate our breakfast. We dug in the dirt and took in the beauty of that profoundly mystical desert forest. My cranium continually expanding as communication to the unseen worlds heightened.

My friend Rich was the land steward, and meditated alone on the land 8 hours a day for a few years. He told me stories of the 4D astral animals that lived there including his astral dog friend. He took me around to all the spots where the astral turtle beings lived and told me of the incredible channeling sessions him and his group had done before the man who bought the land died.

A mysterious story unfolded as he told me more about this man who purchased this land intending to create a 5D star being community. He died of cancer 2 years before my visit. His name was Stuart and he always said that he was from Andromeda too. The most fascinating synchronicity is that he died in March of 2013, precisely the month I first had my own andromedan communication in the back of that taxi which continued into communication with a masculine andromedan spirit guide!

Rich told me that before Stuart died, he said that he would come back as a little Chinese girl. Rich often commented on how Stuart and I would say the same things in the same ways, how we had eerily similar mannerisms. He said that we both had galactic energy and Star Wisdom emanating from us.

One day I jokingly said to Rich that I'd like to bring a dog to the land. He said that dogs scare the astral and wild animals on the land

and that it would be distracting to the work we had to do there. I was a little disheartened at first, but a few days later he told me that Stuart visited him in astral form and let him know that this land actually belonged to me, and that I could do whatever I wanted.

~ ❈ ~

I was sitting outside a coffee shop enjoying the morning sun one day when we were in Albuquerque gathering supplies. An elderly, small man approached me carrying a large tray of crystals - when our eyes met they locked, and I began to giggle. He moved towards me and said: "ah, yes, you are the laughing Buddha!"

Instantly remembering my experiences at the Vipassana centre, my perplexed eyebrows furrow and I say to him: "huh? What do you mean?"

He came towards me even closer, and unpacked a large Quartz crystal the size of my whole hand from wrist to fingertip. He held it out towards me and said: "your grandmother wants you to have this."

I picked the crystal up in my hand and took a closer look. It emanated a pure light energy which filled my awareness with delight. With one smaller piece of quartz coming out of the top end, the whole piece looked like an Eagle. On one of the long surfaces is a small curve as if someone had meditated with it for a very long time while gently stroking it with their thumb. Inside the crystal were two white clouds encapsulating black dots within them… 'hmmm, interesting' I thought, "looks like it takes dirty energy from the world and cleanses it within itself. That's sort of like what I do. Like a plant."

I looked back at the man, as if to say I understood the magic of the crystal. He told me to hang onto it, then said: "I'm going to Tucson to sell some crystals, I think you ought to come with me."

Having no knowledge of US geography I thought Tucson was the name of a crystal store. With little hesitation I hopped into his car.

Soon enough we were on the highway. This man was probably at least 70 years old. His shoulders curved inwards and his body stuttered around as he drove. For a second I wondered if he was good to drive, but I calmed my nervousness by returning to a knowing that this was a divinely guided excursion. He handed me a map, and told me to look up Tucson. I grabbed the map and soon realized Tucson was not a crystal store but a city in Arizona 7 hours away from Albuquerque.

I took a deep breath of acceptance as we embarked on our spontaneous road-trip. If you're wondering, I did ask myself if I was crazy at least once. He told me stories of his work with the native american churches of Turtle Island, but also heinous stories of his past mentioning Alister Crowley. I took it all in and wondered what was to come.

A few hours into our drive, the darkness set upon us and a thunder storm raged all around our small car. Weaving around the snaky roads of the mountains started to feel unsafe, we decided that maybe it was best for us to stop at a motel and wait out the storm for the night. We both cleaned out our pockets and realized we had about $100 between us ~ barely enough for a motel and gas money to get to where we needed to go.

The stormy night wrapped its enveloping darkness around us as we settled into our motel home for the night. He took a brief shower in the bathroom then emerged with a small bud of marijuana in his hand. I always had wild paranoia when I smoked in recreational public settings, so immediately a wave of anxiety came over me.

Something in me also says: "we are in a journey of activation, I surrender to the flow and Trust in the Universe and my Guides."

I agreed with this thought. He loaded up the pipe and I took a sip. The weed whirled my consciousness and energy body into a wavy space and the room filled up with colourful swirls and brilliant lights. He sat in a chair and me on the ground, I watched him intently as he told stories of his journey, both dark and joyful.

When the marijuana's effects got to my head, I became afraid. My fears were irrational to what I have experienced in my life to that point, but I would later unravel why these intense fears were always so deep in my heart and mind.

I was terrified that the CIA was going to bust through the door, arrest me for being a lightworker, kidnap me and sacrifice me in a satanic ritual.

This fear was absurd to me even as I was submersed it in, because it came often and sometimes I'd be so irrationally terrified I'd start to ask people around me if they were going to kill me. Amidst this intense paranoia, I held myself together and continued to ride the experience during which my Higher Self was very present in my consciousness.

At some point he stopped talking all of a sudden, and said to me: "We have to get naked, and I must perform a healing on you."

My thoughts stopped, my breath stopped, everything froze! I mumbled to my own bewildered self: "WHAT?!"

My guides re-assured me, that this was a part of an activation experience, that these experiences will ultimately teach me to trust in my inner voice, hunches and guidance. I think to myself: "well, I'm here already... I might as well go with it."

I took off my clothes timidly, and he took off his. We stood in the middle of this strange motel room… and shared the most innocent hug. We stood there for maybe 20 seconds in a calm, innocent hug in our bare bodies. My suspicions of him making any sort of sexual move towards me dwindled as I relaxed into this strange experience with trust in myself, this strange old man, and the giggling Universe.

He opened his arms then and walked to face my back. Then he opened his mouth and made the most intense, ethereal, ancient tone, "Oooooohhmm…"

He mentioned to me that this is the sound of Source, the ancient Ohm which takes us Home. He stood an arms length behind me and chanted this long enchanting Ohm into all of my chakras, beginning with crown, reverberating Opening and Activation into them as he moved down to my root chakra.

He then moved to the front side of my body and did the same, but from my root chakra up to my crown. I felt my microcosmic orbit which usually rotated through the central channel of my body up the back and down the front, suddenly stop spinning. I reacted in fear thinking: "Oh my! He's stealing my soul!"

But then I calmed myself and felt the spin of my microcosmic orbit actually reverse polarity and begin to spin the opposite way, up the front, down the back.

My taoist ancestors chimed in excitedly: "Well done Xi! This is how you reverse your microcosmic orbit, to integrate new energies and frequencies, to clear out discordant energies, to help you in your Activation process."

Many years later I met a beloved soul brother who told me that in the ancient Mexican traditions of shamanism, initiates often received initiations and activations from elders in the nude. The process of reversing the microcosmic orbit is also a hidden key to embodying breatharianism and eternal youth, known in the eastern traditions as the water path. So indeed this was an activation.

When this session was finished, the old man started speaking in tongues. The sound bounced off the multidimensional light-scape of the room and felt very warm, loving and joyful to me. He said, "You are helping me remember a language which I've not spoken in a million years!"

He then passed out on one of the two twin sized beds in the motel room. I went and lied down in the other bed, body still shimmering from the activating frequencies of the sound healing and all the fear and excitement that rumbled through our night.

Upon rising in the morning, he could not remember any that which happened the night before. I thought this was very curious but I didn't implore. I took note that the CIA agents did not bust down the door, that I did not get kidnapped nor sacrificed in a satanic ritual. Nothing bad happened to me, yet I was so inundated by my irrational fears in those moments last night.

We arrived in Tucson and things did not go as planned, we got into a disagreement and he left me in front of Galactic Centre, a starseed art gallery in Tucson. 5 minutes after this had happened, I met a man who looked like Jesus in front of Galactic Centre. I told him what had happened to me and he agreed to take me back to Albuquerque, since he was on his way to southern Colorado anyway.

~ ✾ ~

When I returned to Albuquerque, I realized that the communication between my Galactic team--my friends who were invisible to the physical realm had greatly heightened. I learned to sing the Galactic

Ohm and started to actively work with energy fields through intention (imagination aka Light) and Sound.

I asked my team again what "sector" of the Mission I am in

They replied: "Healthcare."

I asked what my title was

They replied: "Self-Healing & Galactivation Guide."

My return to Albuquerque was brief as I soon remembered I was still completely depleted in funds. My whole trip lasted just under 2 months yet I had completely shifted. I took a bus back to Montreal in late June and was determined to hang on to these new energies and frequencies I had freshly integrated into my system.

I tried really hard to fall back into the life I had once lived in Montreal too, a life of freedom and music with not a care in the world even if it were to end tomorrow. I was awakened to the depression of the masses but not yet to the heinous crimes committed against Humanity and the Earth on a Cosmic level.

I went to several parties, but I noticed I was no longer dancing and enjoying the endless nights of booming music amongst hundreds of boozed and drugged out people. At some point in my journey, this was so refreshing to see people not pent up in their cubicles… But now I was beginning to see that this box of booming music was nothing more than an escape, another box, a temporary sense of freedom which enabled a lack of motivation to make real shifts in life and reality.

One night in September I pulled some tarot cards, and from my reading it was very clear that my time in Montreal was coming to an end and that I was meant to move back to my parents' home in Alliston, Ontario. I pretended not to notice the deeper meaning of this reading because a part of me was very fond of living there. It didn't take long for Spirit to create very uncomfortable situations that very quickly bounced me out of the city and by Christmas I was back home at my parent's house.

CHAPTER 4

Shamanic Initiation

Life in my parents' house was simple, full of solitude. For the survival of my joy, I built myself a fortress of my own vibration within which I felt comfortable. When I was alone, the only thing that mattered to me was the embodiment of my spirit and the Shifting of my Vibration.

At this point I was still pretty new at perceiving the presence of my galactic team, which was always present and in communication with me. To my awareness it just seemed like a part of my own imagination sending me messages and reminders throughout the day. My entire moment to moment life was devoted to what I perceived as "Mission Heaven on Earth."

Walking my dog became an exercise in seeing how much better life could be if more social structures were created in the small town subdivisions. Dog parks, gazebos, a stage for talent sharing in the public parks. I started envisioning how much sweeter life would be if more families were outside hanging out together, planting communal gardens and creating beautiful land-art.

Inside my small room in my parents house, I shifted the vibration of my room so much it felt like a bio-light-ship. I spent hours and hours meditating, listening to Quantum healing radio shows about the awakening, star-seeds, the quantum reality...

Looking back at this time, I was doing nothing but shifting my vibration in every way possible like it was my full time job. I ate mostly raw foods, slept as much as I could, and swam in my own little universe full of ETs, magic, joy and love.

For a few months, this spring was a period of subconscious activation living inside my little room in my Chinese parents' house. Dream-time was very active and multiple times a day I would find myself swimming in a different vibration from other people. For a period of 2 weeks I received nightly visitations from Star people of all colours and creeds. I dreamt about many things that would unfold over the following 3-5 years.

In one dream, Cumberbatch who played Sherlock Holmes in the BBC series came in a hyperspace-craft to invite me to travel dimensions with him. He showed me how to tunnel through stargates, then said to me in a very Holmes-like stern voice: "Xi, you have very many missions to fulfill in this life-time, so try not to allow emotional distractions to deter you, and when in times of need, call on your inner Sherlock!" ... I had this dream a year before Dr. Strange came out!

In another dream I was in a higher-dimensional light & sound science lab in the middle of hyper-space. Somehow I knew I was a 7-9th dimensional andromedan geneticist. This is one of my higher-dimensional selves now merging with my 3D self.

This aspect of self works with light and sound to create, alter and advance DNA, and played a part in creating the DNA files infused into the ethers allowing starseeds to incarnate on Earth with their gifts in tact. Little USB drives filled with information for the starseeds to access at a later time. This is the aspect of self that works with Starseeds in activating and remembering their soul mission.

In another dream, I was visited by a group of ETs, blue-skinned, black-skinned and feline beings. They brought me into their dimensions and showed me a vision of a moment in the future our Earthling-Starseed family would be anchoring in a community of healers, leaders and teachers, building Star Being Training Facilities.

In yet other dreams, I was shown the light-sound geometric configurations of the spirits of many plant medicines, like psilocybin mushrooms and ayahuasca, and also shown that they were brought to Earth from various star-systems to assist in the Starseed missions.

This gave me a really deep and different context in relating to plant medicines than many other people have, especially some traditional shamans. When I exchange with these plant medicine spirits, I truly feel a great camaraderie with them despite not being native american nor having experienced that many ceremonies.

It's an even deeper level of belonging and knowingness than most humans can know. I say this to share with you a new and profound way starseeds can relate to this reality that may seem extraordinary or extravagant to most people. But grasping and integrating these deep and profound ways of relating to this reality is also how we embrace the fact that we are starseeds, aka ETs on Earth! The reverse ego is still an ego and not owning any part of us afraid of being too "big" or ridiculed is still an ego of fear, which doesn't allow us to accept who we Truly are.

~ ✿ ~

Around this time in the spring of 2015, I found myself crying in utter despair at length and often. Most of the time it wasn't triggered by any particular event at all. And after the release, I'd be relieved of whatever build up it was and return to my regular, fairy-like state of being. When the snow began to melt, I started to realize the correlation between the emotional melt-downs and the suppression of how I truly felt about the suffrage in the World.

I felt my lower belly and back constantly bloated and achy. My legs seemed hollow, as if the weight in my belly were too heavy for them to bear or like the energy stuck there had no way to reach the ground.

I woke one morning wrapped in my green foliage bed sheets embedded with small, bright yellow flowers. I always loved them because they provoked the feeling of waking amongst the lively canvas of the jungle. The sun tenderly caressed everything, leaving golden shimmers through the blinds. I straightened my body and closed my eyes again - not ready to get out of my warm cocoon just yet.

I gently scanned my body with my awareness, an activity which becomes the healing healer's default state in relaxation. I sensed a tightness around my pelvis and as I focused a little more on the region of my ovaries, I saw in their places giant metal gears, covered in cobwebs, fraught with rust. It felt as if they were brittle yet heavy, like they'd slept for a millennia.

I continued to find myself in a similar discomfort and even agony. I practiced every holistic spiritual healing practice under the sun - reiki, meditation, yoga, breath work, psychedelics… you name it. Every day was another spiral deeper into the healing game, and even though I was learning a heck of a lot and gaining plenty of insights into my body, I just wasn't getting to the bottom of my suffering. That was a source of great hopelessness.

I walked out into the woods one day very distraught. I felt all the world's healing as a burden on my own shoulders and all the world's suffering in my own womb. I limped my way into the dense woods, fell to my knees, and screamed at the top of my lungs to an unseen mother: "Please! MOM! Take me back! I'm sorry! Have you given up on me? What do I do? I want to be with you. Please help me…"

I felt my body begin to move almost on its own volition. I could feel the presence of a kind feminine spirit guiding me. A small river ran through this forest behind the subdivision where I lived, and as I moved towards it everything shimmered just a touch more than usual. A dream-like ambiance pervaded the space all around me.

I arrived by the river and continued to walk along the side, with each step I was becoming more inebriated by the freshness and delight of the forest. The hypnagogic quality of my experience deepened as I approached a section of the river where a small island split the stream in two and then rejoined again. I felt my body gravitate toward this spot moved by an unseen force, my mind a curious be-wondered witness.

Five steps before the edge of the river, I felt the space around me shift as if I had entered a bubble of air that is a different density than before. The subtle shift in ambiance was not alarming to me, but a marvellous sparkle of magic I had grown accustomed to in my adventures in the forest. In my ears danced a steady, bubbling trickle that tickled at my heart. My eyes gently gazed towards the small island from which a warmth seemed to emanate.

In the stillness of this moment, again I felt the presence of a feminine, sweet, gentle and kind River spirit. She began to communicate to me. She wrapped me in a cocoon of comfort and compassion and showed me images in my mind's eye of how she saw the children living in the subdivision, eyes glazed over their television and iPhones. Subconscious discomfort, confinement and disconnectivity plagued the houses of the suburb nearby.

I felt an immense grief and anger as she beckoned me to dive deep into my belly into my own ocean of feeling, that somewhere within myself I have seen this too. She said the children of Earth will heal and find true peace and happiness, only if they return to play in the belly of their mother… in the forests, in the rivers, mountains and lakes.

My awareness zoomed back into the forest, to all the budding trees that surrounded me, all interconnected, all alive. The River Spirit guided my body to another spot on top of a hill where a gentle breeze washed over my shivering body, a brilliant energy of unconditional love and inspiration. Then my senses became quiet. "Go to the rainforest my dear, you shall find your healing there."

Let us bring awareness to the reality of extra-sensory perception, available to us not only on mind-altering substances but all the time. Our gift of language has betrayed us, leading us to believe that anything it cannot describe or don't yet have words for, isn't real. Our society acts quickly to label anything as a "mental illness," with selling drugs for money as their only motivation.

I had to experience what it means to play in Her belly. I needed direct communion with Madre Tierra, Pachamama, the divine mother spirit of our Earth. I gave the thought a few weeks, during which nights I had many dreams of rich jungle foliage, ancient amazonian flowers, and rummaging through the dense foliage laughing as a joyful child.

~ ✾ ~

Flash forward a few months, I embarked on a pilgrimage to Costa Rica. My landing was a yoga retreat centre a friend of ours worked in. Little did I know that this was only the beginning of my passage.

Within a week of arriving, I had a dream. A green goddess came to me and informed me that I was becoming a "shaman." Upon awakening from this dream, I walked into the lobby to find the gardener talking about Ayahuasca.

When the grizzly loving man turned around to point to the vine growing in the garden, he exclaimed: "… it's gone!" The few of us ran towards the location of the missing vines. We found the tree that was carrying the vine lying sideways on the ground.

He invited us to harvest the vines, and bring them back to his humble plant nursery in the valley under Diamante Mountain. In the days that followed, we were blessedly steamed by the aroma of the vines from our harvest cooking underneath the open-air bunk where we slept.

In the community, a shaman was facilitating a ceremony that coming weekend, this was the portal into my first communion with the plant medicine. Up to this point in my life, I had heard about ayahuasca and various sorts of psychedelic medicines but never felt a strong desire to seek it out or partake in ceremony.

My first ceremony was very gentle and sweet. I felt the presence of Ayahuasca's spirit. Nearing the end of the ceremony, she came to me holding a box and told me this represents my initiation into carrying the Sacred Wisdom of the Womb. It took me many more years to unpack this Gift.

One day I was feeling a strong call to partake in the medicine by myself. Having a skilled and trained facilitator when journeying with advanced psychedelic plants is extremely important! I received a *very clear* affirmation from Nature which I will describe here; this confirmation was the only reason I proceeded.

So lying in bed one night, I exclaimed in my mind's voice: "Spirit, if I'm really meant to climb up that sacred mountain to drink Ayahuasca by myself, give me a sign! As soon as this thought left my brain, I heard a massive, deep rumbling sound come from outside! It was too dark to see anything then. Waking up the next morning, I found the result of a massive mudslide! Clearly etched in the rock and mud on one entire side of the mountain was the face of an old bearded sage.

The mountain showed me his face! I exclaimed in joy. I went to the gardener's house and asked him for a jar of medicine that he had cooked from the vines we salvaged together. He was hesitant. I told him about the mountain's confirmation and he decided this matter was out of his jurisdiction.

He flipped a coin. Soon enough I was hiking up a very tall mountain, a 20kg pack on my back, and a beautiful jar of ayahuasca in my hand. The first 10 minutes going up hill out of the community I felt so tired I thought I'd never make it. I can still hardly believe I made it up a whole mountain with this pack I felt as heavy as me. Truly the only limitation is our mind.

I hiked for three days before I found the spot. It was midday when I began preparations for my ceremony. I set my altar space in a bamboo gazebo surrounded by jungle vegetation with the sound of a waterfall flowing nearby. I whispered my prayers and settled into my first drink of the medicine.

Within an hour the sensational boundary of my cranium expanded, my vision grew sparkles as all of Life became prominent and in communication… I was brilliant and ecstatic to be alive. As alive as the singing bumblebee gently kissing my shoulder. As alive as the creek rumbling forever. As alive as the tall blooming trees, reverberating with magnetic life force, singing a grand opera only heard with spiritual ears…

I took off my clothes and jumped into a standing pool, meters away the water plummeted down into the cataract below. The crystalline coolness of the water enveloped my whole being. I became a water spirit, dancing, spiralling, whirling, singing.

I looked up towards the sky and tens of hawks encircled me in geometric formations against the majestic mountain… I spotted a dragonfly whizzing beneath the hawks and began to sing to him. He responded to the vibrations carrying my voice on the pixels of space that connected him and I as he altered his course each time I altered my tone.

I squealed in excitement like a young child noticing our visceral connection, forgetting the energetic nature of our dance together. He stumbled and almost fell out of the sky. I giggled: "Sorry dude! My bad! I got excited…"

Feeling drawn towards the waterfall, I swam towards it. The creek that babbled through my experience ran over some giant boulders which perched majestically overlooking the 70ft waterfall. I looked over a big boulder suspended over the canyon… amazing lush greenness was all I could see, all of it pulsing with life and consciousness. I climbed unto this boulder, he had been sun-bathing all day and the warmth of its surface relaxed my butt.

This is Earth. I'm a human. I'm alive, here. I love this… I love this boulder… I love these Eagles, I love the entire canvas of trees and water and clouds… These thoughts rushed through my entire body as the weight I'd been carrying in my belly cracked open and plummeted through my legs, falling, falling down with the waterfall…

The booming thunderous voice of the waterfall carried a hundred years of disconnection from our Mother and the pain that this has caused into the cleansing waters. My thighs wobbled and twitched incessantly and my feet grew hot as this tremendous amount of energy rushed from my hips, a freshly broken dam… I felt such an immense joy come over me as I realized I was living the moment I had prayed for all my life unknowingly.

The sensation of energy streaming down into the waterfall continued for a little while. The sun continued to gleam upon my face and body, I glowed in warmth and contentment. As the sensations began to subside, I felt the presence of a being standing a few feet behind me, a familiar invisible friend. My guardian angel who feels to be a family member from a distant star-system. He enveloped me with an overwhelming feeling of unconditional love and perfect alright-ness…

Coming off the boulder I realize the effects of the medicine were wearing off and it was already late afternoon. I made a fire and gathered some plantains to roast as I prepared to have another drink at night.

Back aboard the bamboo gazebo, night had fallen upon me. Life roared on around me, crickets, ruffling leaves, birds… I knew that a night-time experience would be much different.

An hour or so after the first glass, the first sensations of inebriation became evident. My hands were tingling and a faint kaleidoscopic red, green, and blue grid overlaid everything. I laid down on my soft pallet and entered into a deep state of meditation. A distinct, familiar presence was felt: a team of multidimensional healing technicians who remain mostly unseen visually.

The beings from my innerverse began to move my body as I experienced tremors and contortions. Old emotions and memories of all sorts began to emerge in my thoughts as their corresponding place of storage in my body would light up in sensation.

I saw images of heinous violent crimes committed against my village and my children. A tremendous love and steadfastness filled my chest and forgiveness replaced the ancient fear and hatred. In my trance I saw thousands of fairies and goblins prancing around my organs and insides with scrubbers and cleaning supplies.

I opened my eyes just a peak and saw my grandmother standing in the corner of the ceiling, I realized that through my body I was healing these traumas of my ancestors.

The technicians took control of my air-way, in me a grateful surrender of trust in their gentle care. As I breathed deep into my belly, I saw black clouds gathering the darkness that collected there. As I released the breath, a golden light took out all that no longer served me. I felt really nauseous as I released these feelings and ancient memories of scarcity and fear. I threw up over the edge of the gazebo, squeezing every ounce of the dankness out of me. I whispered prayers of gratitude.

A month later I'm in North America again, back in a small rural city northwest of Toronto. The world I remembered remained mostly unchanged. The orange-suited men who climb the cement towers are still the same, they make an awful ruckus under the power lines that gave me a headache. The people walking by me in the grocery store are doing their best to repress their inner fairy, yet dying to experience the REALity I now know existed just beyond their perception.

In the parking lot of Costco I have a panic attack. As I look to my right, I see an obese man carrying a family pack of hot-dogs and soda to his car with sadness bursting at the seams of his body. I prayed for him to discover the babbling creek and the whizzing dragonfly songs… To my left the cement building stands vehemently on the cement parking lot surrounded by cement poles and glaring white lights.

I panicked in the powerlessness of my inability to spontaneously manifest fruit trees and flowering vines to put in its place. How did reality become this way? Who designed this thing? Who is this designed for? How could everyone continue on in a hazy depression? What can I do? What can I do? What can I do?

CHAPTER 5

Defense Against the Dark Arts

In the months that came after my journey to Costa Rica, many gifts and skills began to activate. It seemed that much more of myself had "un-zipped" in those ceremonies with ayahuasca than I was aware of. I began to see the energetic make up of the human body, as well as blockages, distortions and damage that the sickness caused.

It was deep and rampant in almost everyone. The distortions, programming and traumas influenced the way people lived and expressed themselves in a real and fundamental way. It came as no surprise though… separated from nature, zapped by electricity, poisoned by processed foods and chemical injections… it's a miracle that these bodies are still alive.

My training continued in the rustling concrete jungle, as my guides would incessantly tell me to go to the shopping mall to sharpen my psychic abilities. It was difficult to accept, but I realized that this was my warrior training. And in order to help the masses, I had to lucidly understand the inner workings of human energy systems inside the false matrix.

I sat in the shopping mall and also in subway trains and coffee shops, scanning the energy systems of the people, the environment, everything. I began to see all the mind control programming, etheric implants and entities, genetic degradation to the geometry of their life expression… It was so much to swallow, yet the Truth was exposed through seeing with my own lucid eyes. And in order to fulfill my mission, I had to keep my eyes wide open and process all the information.

I took a couple months of rest and integration time, and by March the weight of the Great Sickness was piling up again. I had to continue to cultivate my extra-sensory perception, which made trying to work a part-time job an impossible task.

I wasn't channeling enough joy to spark aliveness and imagination in every being in my neighborhood, so I started to feel worthless, moody and depressed. Even still, I knew deep inside me Spirit was kindly giving me this time of rest to regather my strength after the recent pilgrimage.

Around this time I discovered the intensity of the child and sex trafficking issue on Earth. I learned that opening my eyes meant going deep, and this means not just as deep as I am comfortable but going as deep as the Truth takes me. This Truth disclosed a huge problem on Earth where adults are stealing young children, as little as infants, and selling them into the sex trade, which was supported by the wealthiest of elites.

It was easy to predict that the next lesson in my school of life was to discover the multi-dimensional reasons these heinous rituals and abductions happened on Earth, and how my awareness and psychic skills can be of service to its healing.

In March 2017 my journey with Ayahuasca continued to my surprise in Canada. One morning I had a dream of being in a dark room which held child ritual sacrifices and sex abuse. In my dream I was playing my medicine drum and singing icaros (shamanic songs), clearing the energy, and asking for forgiveness and the light to return.

The morning I awoke from this dream, I was greeted by an invitation to a weekend of ceremonies.

The universe and the web of life has its way of orchestrating in sublime ways. My guides told me that they waited as long as they could to tell me about these dark issues, protecting my innocence and purity. As soon as they showed me, they also provided me with my Medicine I can use to help. And as if an answer to my questions surrounding the "evils" of this world, I was taken to both ends of light and darkness.

~ ❀ ~

I sat on my pallet in a cozy living room by a wall of tall windows; a row of tall pine trees in a blooming protective stance encircled me and the full moon was shining gracefully upon my body. There were only 2 other people in the room: an older woman, Grandmother Waterfall, who was housing us and our shaman. There were many others who had planned to attend this ceremony, but none of them made it. This was a ceremony for me.

Adorned by the most beautiful feather head-dress, the shining one danced, drummed, rattled and sang through the night, reverberating purity and love, guiding me into a deep, cosmic space. I flew to the Source of Creation. I opened my eyes as a pure, joyful young child, and the shaman seemed to be the creator itself smiling at me. As if she had just finished sculpting my body and soul, she smiled lovingly and proudly at me, a beautiful creation…

I felt like a beautiful creation by the hand of God, and she was smiling at me, happy with what she had just created. I zoomed out into the universe and felt the love between the universe and the Earth, and the Earth with all its children. It was palpable.

Drinking the Nourishment of these feelings, I realized that I was being prepared for a long journey through the underworld. Soon after this realization I was plunged into the consciousness of John Podesta, a well known figurehead of the elite child trafficking rings.

I flew into this dark place, holding my connection to my Divinity and Grace, finding him sitting there in the middle of a dark room encircled by 7 other shamans. They wore skin of rainbow colours and ceremony garments from all different galactic cultures. John was the only participant of his own ayahuasca journey, holding a cup of medicine in his hands.

Before I could contest, my spirit flew into the cup as he drank it. Holding onto my connection to the Source, I entered his consciousness to help him reconcile from disconnection and sickness.

I saw a strangled constriction, rage and confusion, such a fear of lack and death that leads one to siphon the most innocent and perfect of life energy in the most heinous way. I had to embody perfect unconditional love, forgiveness and acceptance then in that moment. I felt I had merged with the presence of the Divine Mother. As if I was the medicine, I whispered to him, would you like to come home?

He faced the goddess, we met eye to eye. My only wish was for him to acknowledge his true desire: union with Life itself. His consciousness glitched and struggled, as if the original programs of soul had been completely hijacked and corrupted. All the while the backdrop of our meeting was the cosmic sky, a perpetual reverberation of only Love. After what felt like hours of struggle, he finally surrendered. Love won.

Some time through the ceremony, the shaman asked me: "would you sing us a song?" I steadied my shivering body quivering in delight, joyful to receive such a pleasant request. I closed my eyes, and for the first time in my life I felt my spirit move up into my soul-star chakra 8 inches above my head. I felt a distinctly unique vibration enter my body and the most exquisite of songs flowed out of my mouth.

I was shown that these songs are from the Angelic realm. They hold the vibrations of perfect Divine Love & Coherence and hold the power to restore this Love and Coherence to any distortions of space and geometries in all dimensions. I acquired the download I needed to fulfill the dream leading up to the ceremony.

Through reading the Don Juan books by Carlos Casteneda, I learned that this kind of crossing between the Dreaming and Waking world is the natural reality of the Shaman.

The issues of sexual distortions, child trafficking and sex abuse was heavy on my mind. These were the most severe parts of the sickness, but sexual corruption is abundantly clear even in the way sex is portrayed in the media. Stealing innocence whether through direct physical abuse or psychological assault through media programming is on the same spectrum of distorting purity, truth and love.

Sexuality is the basis of creation, it is pure creative energy. Thus the corruption of sexuality is the corruption of creativity and hence the robbery of life and of reality itself. The sickness is one of separation from Creation, from Life itself.

The world, stricken with an imperceptible sickness that blinds one from recognizing its vile hold until the death of a planet, is seen in the catastrophic suffering and disappearance of life.

We are beautiful beyond our knowing, intelligent and powerful beyond our nuclear weapons and games of deception, magical beyond what is currently imaginable. We are equipped with the ancient knowledge that still lives in the elders, the healers, the mystics and the plants. We can return to our grand co-creation with creation itself. All we need is to Choose.

~ ✽ ~

A couple of months after the initial ceremony with this particular shaman, I received a call from him. He informed me that he sat with divine mother Ayahuasca by himself a few days ago. This was his personal training ceremony, so he took 4 doses. He told me that when he was at the peak of this journey there by the river, a tipi appeared in his visions.

When he entered the tipi, he saw me sitting there in my full ceremonial regalia. He saw me singing and performing healing for others in this tipi, and that it looked like I have "been around the block a few times." Coming out of this journey he decided to call me and invite me to become his student.

Of course at the time I was thrilled. I immediately accepted and continued to sit in 17 ceremonies with him for the rest of 2017. He asked me to build him a Tipi so he can come and hold ceremonies in it on my birthday. I gathered the money necessary through applying for several local grants.

My experience inside these ceremonies were both incredibly terrifying and full of satisfying soul remembrance and embodiment. It was where I learned that my theories about interdimensional attacks during childhood are true. Journeying with the panther, the hummingbird, coyote and bear, I flew into the different dimensions of time-space to see my childhood home ravaged by open negative portals and demonic entities.

I learned so intimately that our bodies are not just merely physical. I learned that consciousness, and not just that which we would perceive to be 'our own', of all dimensions permeate our bodies. And from this perspective, entities, fragments and negative energies of traumatized places and land greatly affect our experience of consciousness inside our body.

Those full-on nights bent over a bucket, scrubbing the cells and energetic structures of my insides clean, I saw a lot. I saw the directed energy weapons intending to keep my starseed DNA from firing. I saw the entities who made deals with the big boss to burrow into my ovaries to keep me from ever becoming empowered in my creativity. I saw the negative portals and beings which drove my parents nearly mad in order to destroy my foundation of love.

On top of my personal stuff, these ceremonies always lead into a period of collective grid and consciousness clearing too. It started with my hometown, seeing into the astral plane and how the angry spirits of the native people that were slaughtered and displaced influenced the local drug and alcohol addiction problems. I saw the artificial and chemical additives in food and pharmaceuticals leaving extremely disruptive and corrupting miasma in energy bodies.

In the shamanic perspective of reality everything has consciousness, and we can access and experience it through projecting our own consciousness towards it. Through this method of getting to know the reality directly from our own inner eyes, we recognize that source-disconnected consciousness and fragments often carry a frequency which feels harmful to us.

In the energetic cellular level of reality, parasitism creates feelings of terror, anger, frustration, depression, constriction and trauma.

Often times these are the energies which are food and the needed environment for these energetic parasites to survive.

In one perspective, these parasites are the by-product of our disconnected state. Food left out to rot will grow mold and maggots. Our energy body and consciousness disconnected from our Source of Divinity and Love, which isn't just centrally located inside our head but in fact permeates our body, will attract and develop energetic parasites too.

I recognized that these deep lucid eye-opening learning experiences were preparing me to become a guide for others to heal from this rampant planetary pandemic. Especially to be able to translate these ideas and understandings into a language which every human can understand and receive.

It was important for me to remember that I have come here for All of Humanity and this living Planet. The intelligence of a divine creator being is infinitely capable of creating solutions in multiple frequency bands simultaneously. It is a joyful game. All I had to do was allow it to anchor and embody through my entire vessel, through purging and healing myself entirely.

~ ❀ ~

The summer of 2017 marked the beginning of a brand new leg of my journey, as the subtle realities of entities, implants and geometric field distortions had become my new normal. I discovered the work of a beloved brother, Eric Raines, on a radio show focussing on the reality of what he refers to as the Parasitic Construct.

Listening to this brother talk so assuredly on the existence of the invisible controllers of humanity, yet also joyfully about the hope and empowerment that comes from activating our own super powers and reclaiming our sovereignty, rang so true to my spirit! I attended his advanced energy healing retreat in Mt. Shasta.

The retreat included 3 hours of daily practice, a conglomeration of Qi-Gong, Yoga and Breathwork ~ doing 3 hours of soul-body alignment exercises every morning in the sacred activation zone of Mt. Shasta catapulted my consciousness into the presence of a new Higher Aspect of self. I started becoming a vibration of self that was still new to me, yet so familiar and ancient.

This part of my self wore a cloak made of full-spectrum void energy, at oneness with the fabric of reality in the multidimensional landscapes which made me invisible in the higher dimensional realms. I am calm, in a deep connection and relationship with Source, and empowered and mandated by all of Divinity to clear and reconnect all back to Source.

At this I could only access this vibration of myself through hours of breathwork and practice, and only have access to her for focussed periods of time. When my awareness left to do other tasks, I would return to my previous level of consciousness forgetting about her altogether.

However through more focussed time of practice and integration, she started to walk-in to my body through my crown down into my vessel, where she has become a more integrated aspect of my earth personality.

Since this time, many other higher aspects of self has also integrated into my vessel, a process I understand now as soul integration and embodiment. The process is akin to a higher self walk-in, where disincarnate high vibrational aspects of self are finally able to incarnate as we raise the vibrations of our consciousness and vessel.

These aspects of self naturally remember certain schools of knowledge, skills, intel and their missions as they are connected to the field of oneness undisturbed by amnesia. Or simply, we are reaching our awareness beyond earthly amnesia, to remember that which we always knew before we were born.

One afternoon we were trading sessions with other participants of the retreat, practicing our psychic capabilities. My partner laid on the floor and I sat on my knees beside him. As I closed my eyes to my surprise I was able to see an etheric body floating above him. Immediately I knew that this etheric body was connected to some of my patient's DNA that had been harvested to create cyborg soldiers during the galactic war.

I asked my higher self, what do I do? And immediately I knew to de-activate the DNA connected to this cyborg, bring back any pieces of his spirit that was connected to it, and send the rest of it to Source. As I did this, I felt a lot of energy rush in and return into my patient's heart and at the exact same time he gasped for air! He experienced the return of his genetic and spirit energies and said his heart was very much more open and he felt more at peace.

I'd say this was one of the first visceral experiences of performing multidimensional healing on another person without the presence of a psychedelic plant medicine. Since then, my psychic senses and claircognizance continue to blossom.

This activation initiated me into fully participating in cleaning and restoring Divine Coherence in the multidimensional fields of Reality. As physicality precipitates down from the higher dimensions, this way of lightwork allow us to shift and heal the geometries of the higher dimensions in order to manifest the New Earth in the physical reality.

~ ❀ ~

As you can imagine, opening up the third-eye and activating my psychic senses in this way completely shifted the way I viewed the world and my role within it. It also greatly enhanced my self-healing as I was no longer sending "healing energy" in ignorance - I knew exactly what I was transmuting. This also led me into way more adventurous journeys in my innerverse, as collective clearing missions began to show up regularly.

These skills also allowed me to explore something I had often been suspicious of in those days. I had a really difficult time in high school, as this twisted and odd energy permeated my family home. My mother would often go into a senseless rage, spewing verbal knives of hurt and destruction upon my gentle spirit. At the worst of it, she told me to just go die.

It's important to know that my mother and I had a very close relationship in my childhood, and she's truly an incredible woman. I suspected that something was driving her to act in this way, and only after these activations of my third eye was I able to truly figure out why this was happening. This energy turned into an ugly eating disorder and severe depression that almost took my life.

Through these psychic activations, I looked back in time through the Quantum reality and was clearly shown the astral activities surrounding my home and the entities that worked through unsuspecting people around me. The people around me would be loving and normal sometimes, then without any provocation spur into a crazy rage and yell hurtful things at me like "you can go die" or "you are useless."

This happened multiple times a week. When I would just be sitting in my room, my door would bust open and I would receive these sorts of insanely energetically charged remarks.

Of course at the time, these experiences left me distraught in tears. In dealing with this extremely turbulent emotional terrain I developed illnesses, which I now know were due to entities and loosh harvesting portals in the astral plane.

However nasty these attacks were, usually the dark plans of the insidious ones backfire. In our resilience, when we experience these attacks, they end up shaking us awake and making us stronger in the long run. They provide us Luminous Starseeds the fertile soil and righteous rage to ultimately fulfill our Destiny.

In psychic-sight I see the distorted light fields, energy weapons and nasty entities which created a living hell in my bedroom. In the mundane physical reality, I was consumed by Anorexia and Bulimia. But when my gifts came online, I was able to locate and remove the entities that encouraged me to harm myself while remarking how dumb and worthless I was. I did once believe these were my own thoughts.

In this family home we had taken a family portrait. Before I left on this journey, I clearly remember seeing this photo and being so disturbed by it, as you can clearly see a demonic energy grabbing my arm through her body.

The incredible thing is that after I returned home for a visit after participating in genetic healing work with ayahuasca and multidimensional energy, this demonic energy inside the portrait disappeared and even my family acted differently. They were showing signs of interest in spiritual things and their energy towards me became much lighter and more welcoming.

These are lofty intuitive feelings, the truth behind them was too scary for most of me to accept and integrate for a very long time. My familiar Jupiter, the wizard cat, took me on a shamanic dream journey which brought deep clarity and reconciliation.

Dream :: I'm floating, gliding and traveling in the air between treetops of beautiful redwoods riding on my kitty Juju. The energy was serene, joyful, yet playful and lively. I couldn't see the ground from here but I was supported by an abundance of prana and love of the trees.

I felt that since the beginning of my life my parents tried to tell me to be a certain way that wasn't true to my soul. They wanted me to turn my magic off and live in boredom on the ground with them. I could perceive inside this dream that it wasn't really them but something insidious in the interdimensional space that was controlling everyone.

I grew up unable to do the mundane things because my perception was filled with magic which was fun and dear to me, and this made me an outcast in my own physical family and society. Yet even though there was magic just beneath the surface of my perception, there was also something off kilter and evil, too. It was an invisible force, inside of people and all around them.

This force influenced people to lose their spark, to live in a daze, a state they know as normal. And it made people act mean towards me, even my own family. It made them yell at me to be normal too, to lose my spark and be like them. But I couldn't. I couldn't give up my magic. So I became the one who flew amongst the tall canyons of redwood trees with my kitty where I couldn't see the ground.

Then Jupiter flew me inside different rooms which appeared on the branches and canopies. In each room we entered, I saw a different scene from my childhood where this dark force had interacted with me, either directly or through family members, teachers, the TV or dreams.

In one room, I felt the presence of my cousin who was pretending to be nice to me. When I saw her body finally she yelled, "Your mother is so ashamed of you, why can't you be like us!" As she yelled angrily, an invisible evil venom spewed from her energy field into mine which caused me to begin to fall down, down, down through the treetops.

I was tumbling into invisible rooms inside the redwood tree, in every room reliving many times where I tried to shut down my magic and my family yelling at me in frustration because I triggered the pain of their own grief in the loss of their own magic.

The invisible insidious force made it known that if I was free and flying amongst magic then I would not be food for it, so it punctured me through my own physical family's hurtful words and thoughts about my very essence.

The depth of this wound allowed some very scary interdimensional entities to enter my being and live inside me, which I wouldn't have been able to notice if I just went to sleep on the ground and ate poisoned and corrupted food like everyone else did.

Jupiter made sure I understood that the dream was teaching me a new frequency/way to sense soul-level and interdimensional trauma and to navigate quantum timeline healing. I gained a clarity with which to integrate my deepest soul fragmentation on this planet and also a new dimension to relate to starseed children here.

Through accepting these higher-dimensional realities, I came to find that these attacks left incredible amounts of miasma and debris inside my body and energy field. As if they knew what my super-powers were, before I could even find them myself they had already dislodged and blocked up the parts of my body and energy bodies which would generate the most Energy and Light. They filled my meridians and chakras with satanic "juices" of nastiness and degradation.

In my early days of clearing and healing from these attacks, I would often be on the floor crying in hopelessness as I truly felt disabled as if I'd never recover. But don't worry, there's a light at the end of this dark tunnel. Not only is total clearing and healing possible, but it's inevitable for our Self and All That Is.

On the surface I was just a teenage girl with an eating disorder, like millions of others who suffered from this common mental illness. But beneath that was a millionfold amount of pain that I can't even begin to explain, that wasn't mine to carry, that was inserted into me with the sole intention of derailing me from ever fulfilling my mission to Restore Divine Harmony in all Dimensions.

I know now that all of these experiences were very important aspects of my Mystery School of Life. Had I not been hospitalized for my eating disorder and anxiety, I would have never seen the terrible state of our "medical system." Had I not withstood the years of psychic assaults in my earlier years, I would have never seen with my own eyes the amount of distortion and damage encased inside our bodies from living inside the false matrix.

These difficult moments in my life were one side of the Bridge. My current mystical and empowered life is the other side. Activating my multidimensional skills of healing and vision and devotedly healing myself enjoined the two sides of the Bridge. Through integrating and embodying higher-dimensional gifts and creating pathways for them to heal and restore wounded parts of myself, I learned to create the New Earth in my own life.

We are so incredibly resilient and as powerful as the Universe Herself. I sit here today feeling joyful, celebrating the Victory which sincerely has set in my Heart. Truly we have already won. As Above, So Below. As Within, So Without. I know within myself that the Dark has lost their grip on my Body and Embodiment Process. And it's only a matter of time when this becomes totally manifest in the external reality as well.

However painful and uncomfortable the healing process can be, restoring Myself to my Divine Luminosity is not only Possible but Inevitable! In each moment, we can Choose to Heal More, Shine Brighter, and Love Deeper!

CHAPTER 6

False Matrix Correction

At the end of 2017, I received a message from my galactic & angelic team that I would be grid-working for some time in Mt. Shasta. An opportunity came to house-sit there for a few months. Last minute the opportunity fell through and I ended up returning home to Ontario for the new year of 2018.

I was guided to get a job. Getting a job was not something I've had to do for the first 5 years of my awakening, so I was very confused and reluctant at first. Yet I recognized this pattern of needing to return to my parents' house for grounding and stability each year, and desired for that cycle to come to an end and become sovereign.

I realized that in order to become sovereign, I need to create pathways of grounded abundance for myself. If I am indeed a fountain of infinite abundance in the higher realms, then this should easily be mirrored in 3D if I am embodied.

A quickly as I surrendered to my path, I found a very interesting well paying job as an organic chef at a holistic addictions recovery centre. My guides told me this was a part of my training and the money will catapult me into my next level of higher-self embodiment on Earth.

When I started working, it became blatantly obvious what the training was about. Remembering that there are many dimensional levels to my mission on Earth, a very grounded one being the transformation of health care systems in mass society, once again I was placed inside it to learn. It was actually quite enjoyable as I discovered I could chopped carrots and banished entities off the recovering addicts at the same time.

The physical nature of the job provided me a way to strengthen my physical vessel, yet staying open in my psychic centres at the same time really anchored these capabilities into the physical for me. The recovery centre was situated way out in the country surrounded by beautiful nature. I had access to the most high quality expensive organic food which aided the strengthening of my physical vessel. I was very happy.

While I was not allowed to chat with the clients about their recovery or spirituality, I was able to gain an up-close and personal assessment of their psychological, energetic and spiritual system. I was also able to witness how the psychic work that I did on the environment and our collective energy fields silently affected their progress and reality.

My employers were pretty spiritual folks who showed us "the secret" at our orientation day, so they knew the kinds of things I was into. I actually really agreed with them that my shamanic knowledge had not been integrated enough to communicate with most of those clients, because I would probably freak them out.

They were supportive enough of my endeavors to say offer me a raise for my added shamanic skills of clearing and keeping the centre clear, and give me their blessing to sing and dance through the house as I pleased while I worked.

It was through this experience I realized that in order to be of assistance to the masses, my beloved human family, I needed to be able to sharpen my diplomatic skills and communicate correctly. Learning to integrate and process multidimensional knowledge, and communicate clearly with all people was now a main subject of study.

Sometimes the higher self of clients would actually ask for my help. This is the only time I operated inside their field. It's important to note that working on people psychically without their permission can actually be dangerous. I generally only sweep and clear things outside of people's form and around them. I sent them packets of energy and light that they can take into their system if they so choose.

This really grounded my psychic gifts and sight into my physical body. Within 2 months I saved up enough money, completed this part of my training, and received intel to sit in a last minute ayahuasca ceremony with a new medicine man in Hamilton, then relocate to Vermont.

~ ❀ ~

Around this time of year, a mutual friend introduced me to Michelle and Kevone who created Activation Coaching, a company that I am now joyfully a part of. Having only seen their faces in facebook pictures, it surprised me to have had such a very vivid dream about them.

In the dream I was in a school room. I was sitting in one of these beige rectangular school desks in a room full of people when all of a sudden in the top ceiling corner of the room appeared two people. They were also sitting at a desk, but this desk was pulsing in and out of reality and on an angle as if they were in a different dimension all together!

It's Michelle and Kevone! Dressed in a black leather coat (like in the Matrix) with black sunglasses in the shape of black swans, they had their arms crossed as if they were very serious. "We are taking you out of the matrix."

~ ✤ ~

Being guided to go to this ayahuasca ceremony in March of 2018 was interesting because I had already felt my time with the medicine coming to an end at least for this phase of my life. I felt I had gotten everything I needed from her in my training to perform multidimensional energy healing for myself and others, and so my relationship with her was shifting. However, I was feeling so guided to be there; of course I obliged.

Sitting in the basement of a very nice new home in a subdivision of a small city, I found myself in circle with 15 mostly young people. The home was well decorated and bright, and the hosts were very sweet and welcoming. There was an excitement and a sense of community in the room already, since most of the participants work regularly with this local medicine man.

When the time approached 10 PM, the lights dimmed and a kind loving small Colombian man sat with his wife and welcomed us into ceremony. They spoke their prayers and their boundaries for their ceremony, then began to pour the drink.

This medicine was not pungent like the one I was used to. It was almost a little sweet. The first 7 hours of the ceremony I was in a space of beauty and bliss, the medicine man recognized my medicine and invited me to participate in holding space with him. I sang many songs and danced and helped the energy move in the room.

Sometime after the second serving of medicine, I brought my singing drum inside. When the medicine man saw this, he honoured me by inviting all the participants to join in a tighter circle as he prepared to share embil, an edible thick paste tobacco medicine which helped us to connect to the dream lines and ground our energy into focus.

He said: "Our sacred sister will share a sacred song with us, and this is the way we will honour her and what comes through her."

This experience itself greatly affected me, because up to this point in my life I have been mostly ridiculed and put down by traditional elders running old paradigm programs deeming my "bad-ass millennial starseed" ways as outrageous and disrespectful. So to be recognized and honored in this way by an elder medicine man truly touched my heart.

After everyone took part in the tobacco medicine, I felt the energy of grace come and I started to channel a beautiful song, carrying the frequencies Divine Mother Gaia as well as activation of the bird tribe and mermaid DNA. I continued to tell several people in the circle about their mystical aspects unfurling. I was so grateful to be able to share my medicine as a part of an ayahuasca ceremony, a medicine that felt so dear to me since my birth name literally means fragrant medicinal tea.

By this time, morning light was peeking through the windows and everyone was coming off of their journey. Most people left the room to get snacks and some were asleep. I was in a very beautiful, serene place, dancing my bead necklace around in the sun. One little part of me was a little confused because I was anticipating something more eventful to happen since I was so guided to be present at this ceremony.

Then I felt a slight tinge of nausea in my belly. One eyebrow perks up, I think to myself: "I wonder what's coming..?" I went to sit back down on my pallet and closed my eyes to meditate.

Immediately I flew up into another dimension. I saw a bright blue portal open up. Three Egyptian fish-headed goddesses and I held this portal open, as what looked like Baphomet was escorted off the face of the planet.

All while this was happening, I was realizing that Baphomet was the representation of the Being behind all the heinous realities of Earth, specifically the demonization, degradation and enslavement of the Goddess, the Mother, the Giver of Life. Baphomet represented the reversal of organic geometries of Life, siphoning pain for its own survival.

If we researched the source of Baphomet, she was actually originally the Goddess of Fertility or simply one representation of the Divine Mother. The goat has symbolized fertility, feminine mysteries and sexuality in many ancient and aboriginal.

This is a deep, ancient level of knowledge which only Angelics, scholars, priests and temples had access to. It is knowledge of the Mechanics of Creation. So when people speak of fallen angelics, to me this is quite literal. There were a high angelic being with power and knowledge of all of Creation, who used this knowledge to gain control over the creation itself.

It is through the control and degradation of the Portal of Life, or the Womb, which allows All of Creation to be hijacked and false realities to be spawn. This is the greatest underlying reason for misogyny, patriarchy, and the degradation of Woman into Demon. We can see this degradation of the Feminine in many religions and cultures.

After this being was escorted back to Source for rehabilitation, I saw a vision of the city. The city represented to me the false matrix of disconnection, and in my vision I was seeing it through what felt like the lens of a memory. It was as if everything in the 3D false matrix reality was truly an echo of a heinous crime of the past, crumbling as we speak.

It would be difficult for the linear conscious mind to understand this intuitive feeling, but I was deeply nourished by the truth that the worst is behind us. That even though lower level astral beings were still running around doing their thing, the big boss has been taken out and handled.

What's left is not a fighting of a war, but cleaning and healing the traumatized bodies, etheric bodies and memory complex of Humanity and Gaia

This experience led me to realize that the most important work we have to do right now is clearing the distorted residue, memories and energy patterns (geometries) of consciousness from having lived through the false matrix out of our multidimensional energy systems.

As Humans are divine creator beings, what is inside of us continues to manifest and perpetuate outside of us. There isn't an external force that can come and change the world for us, because this is our duty as the guardians and children of this planet!

So while many like to argue about politics, and complain about the medical and education systems, what we have to realize is that there is no longer a centralized power of control which is perpetuating the creation of those systems. We are actually continuing the creation of those systems ourselves with the memories and patterns we have of them.

So in order to restructure, clear and fix these cultural and societal systems, we must take on the mantle of responsibility of completely clearing and restoring our Self of all false matrix viruses, belief systems, traumas and victimization.

The clean up is happening in the higher dimensions through galactic and higher forces (higher aspects of our self), but this means we also have to do the work on the Earth plane. It's our job to heal our self, our traumas and subconscious false matrix belief systems and patterns and clean our planet up in 3D! Down here we are the ones perpetuating the false matrix unconsciously, and it's up to every one of us to restore our self back into alignment with Divinity!

CHAPTER 7

Pleiadian Goddess Vortex

You might find this hilarious, that oftentimes Spirit doesn't give me details to a mission until days prior to it's destined occurrence. One such fateful day in March, I started to feel bored and even irritated by my cooking job. I checked in with my guidance and sure enough, I was being guided to leave. I told the company owners I wasn't feeling well and left for the day. Driving through a small, snow-covered country town I decided to stop into a coffee shop.

Sitting inside the coffeeshop pondering over the waves of ecstatic energy communicating to me, I received a text message from a friend of mine whom I haven't spoken to in a long time. He told me that he was in Vermont and that it was time for us to reconnect. I checked in with my guidance and realized that I was to drive there immediately… From Ontario, Canada to Vermont, USA was about an 8 hour drive… It was already 5pm…

I sat inside the coffee shop for another 2 hours before finally succumbing to the incessant knowingness inside that going was the right thing to do. Night had begun to fall. I gassed up my car, packed up a few things and went on my way. As soon as I got in the car on my way to my next mission, the sky opened up. My psychic centers were fully activated and a pleasant festive joy permeated my reality.

This is a feeling I associate with being "online", as it isn't always necessary to be absolutely connected into all my galactic aspects especially when I chop carrots. When I go on these grid work missions, I get tapped into my multidimensional team as well as the light technologies that help me stay lucid, present and clear.

I decided to crash at a friends place in Montreal for the night, so that it would be daylight when I arrived in Vermont. It was the middle of March and heaps of snow still covered the ground. As soon as I drove into the mountain range of a town, I immediately knew that I was inside a Pleiadian Goddess Vortex.

Gorgeous flowing rivers cascaded over the hills of giant rocks and boulders covered in delightful, angelic white snow; the prismatic sunlight warmed my spirit as I drove towards my friends house. To my extending delight, the house was on a hill of a large valley in the centre of a large circle of mountains. The Spirit of the Mountain directly across from the house winked at me and made his presence known.

The mystery commenced shortly after my arrival. The Earth and the Galactics' communication were clearer to me than ever, but the messages were also getting more interesting! I was told that the root chakra of the Earth is going to be shifted for a month or two, as I commence my work at my new post. That it was by no accident that I almost stayed in Mt. Shasta for a few months, but this was delayed and shifted to Lincoln, Vermont.

They shared with me that due to the large amount of interference and false light infiltration in Mt. Shasta and the level of gridwork we were called to do at this time, this was the solution.

Within the first week of me arriving at my new home in Vermont, the first clients that came to me were a couple from North Carolina who had recently completed a channelled book about Authentic Love & Sacred Sexuality with the Pleiadians. During our sessions a part of me would be anchoring and weaving in what felt like a Field of Crystalline light in the frequency of Authentic Love.

First it rippled across the entire atmosphere surrounding the Earth, a crystalline pink and yellow and algae field of energy. Through time I realized that this field of energy was organic and alive and was constantly expanding and learning new skills. I began to use this field of energy to absorb satanic reversal energies whenever I encountered them, and the field would transmute this energy to make itself bigger and stronger! I was then guided to anchor this field into 5G towers.

Feeling into the ancient boulders that graced the land, reading their lines of ancient Light, the stories of this ancient light technology began to come alive. Each day I perched in my healing room with a giant window facing the mountain, I tuned into these boulders.

Each day through tuning into the ancient lines of light, and weaving consciousness into them, I knew I was activating it. I was connecting with my channel of pure consciousness from the Pleiades, beyond time-space, into the technology now so it can be accessible by consciousness and functional in our world.

Through my stone reading and trance journeying work, I discovered many things about this ancient pleiadian technology that I was here to turn on. I understood that it is created outside of timespace which gives it the ability to influence timelines.

I learned that this technology was most likely conceived before the Pleiadians came to Earth either running away from the Draco-reptilians or having made a deal with them. The Pleiadians knew it wasn't time yet for the Light to overcome the evil, so they created this timeline technology to be accessed at a later time when more conscious energy was available in the Cycle of the Cosmos.

At the seeding of this lineage of Cherokees here to this location, they also seeded the blueprint of this crystalline light technology which is powered and navigated with Divine Consciousness. When the time was right cosmologically, it was destined to be discovered and turned on to assist in the Liberation of our Universe from evil.

I continued to learn much more about this technology over the following years through synchronous sessions with starseeds who also worked on bringing this tech to Earth through-out time.

The timeline capabilities of this tech functioned similar to the reality of Mandela effects. I was shown that if it is possible for us to suddenly appear in a new reality or timeline, then it would also be possible for us to mechanize this possibility and drive it with our Divine Creative Consciousness. We would be able to consistently steer humanity into higher and higher timelines, as if by miracles.

Weeks later I met a man at the local native village who introduced himself to me as a Cherokee elder. He approached me because he saw the "Star-being" energies inside me and was curious to know more. He shared with me that he is from the Taygeta star system of the Pleiades and continued to tell me the creation story of his Cherokee people who are native to this land.

He says a long time ago, these giant spiders came from the sky carrying his people down to the Earth. According to the Cherokee people who lived there, the valley which my house was in the middle of was actually created by a Pleiadian Mothership when it landed many moons ago.

Hearing this story from a Cherokee elder from the land simply blew my mind. Talk about confirmation of hunches! Any doubt or fear of being crazy vanished as I became empowered with a new sense of wonder and joy.

~ ❀ ~

It was a very interesting team of people who lived at this house in the centre of the valley, and we were gathering at a very interesting place during a very interesting time. The house was alive and was part of the light technology itself. And when it was "ON," the walls of the house turned colours and lit up in chrome and rainbow sparkles. When this happened, in my psychic eye I would see that the house was situated on top of many leylines, and the energy work that carried on inside the house would act as a template signal, transmitted via the leylines to places our energy was needed.

Every couple of days, our house mates and friends would gather spontaneously and hold space all night in what felt like deep, gridwork ceremonies. We didn't ever plan them nor did we call them that, but it was like our souls knew what we were doing there.

Hans would light the fire, as Bella began to pray and weave lines of light into our space. Jack would start singing and Ken would start the water for tea. I would sit in meditation and watch the shifting of energy to figure out what we were doing, seeing the house transform into a transmission station.

It was March, and according to many occult documents, March to May was a powerful time, and a time the elites planned many satanic ritual parties. Very often late into the night, we begin to weep as we realize we are holding space for the children and people hurting in those situations.

One night in particular during one of our ceremonies, I was sitting on our patterned carpet in front of the fire. In meditation I can almost hear their screams of agony, a whole new level of terror hits me in my stomach. I pull in all the strength and clarity available to me and I sit up straight and breath. I can hear them say: "Don't forget about us. If you forget, then no one will remember us. Then we will be lost. Don't forget about us. Don't forget about us…"

I relayed what I saw, felt and heard to the group, and we all agreed on our shared experience of holding space for the transformation of these disgusting energies. We knew how important it was for us to hold space and send love and support to the children for their healing.

These spontaneous spirit-coordinated moments in time would happen many times a week, each time with different configurations of people, animals and energy, yet they never ceased to amaze me infinitely. Each time these miracle coordinates occurred, we tackled a big collective grid-work mission. Yet on the surface, it just looked like we were enjoying conversations and having a good time.

I always watched the walls of the house turn "on" and transform into myriad cascades of light, as our collective energies moved through the leylines out to transform the world. This never ceased to delight me.

There was always such an ambience of warmth and magic like scenes out of Narnia at times, as the hills of early spring Vermont are still covered with delightful snow. Magical beings in the form of humans showed up to share music, stories, medicine and joy. The magic was so pure, beautiful and plentiful, I was in awe that there still exists a place on Earth where this is a reality.

Giant quartz-filled boulders were spread across the valley, two stood proudly in front of this magical house. The fairies often came to tell me stories of their life here before the Pleiadians came to seed their offspring. The fairies cried in devastation of the ways humans conduct themselves nowadays, completely cut off from magic.

They are afraid of the false matrix crawling into their sacred valley, perhaps one of the last places in North America where magic is still abundant and pure. Hearing these cries, I cried with them. In desperation and frustration, I knew these feelings were the appropriate response in a moment like this.

I became totally enchanted by the Beauty and Magic abundant in the natural realms of the Earth. It's a force beyond just Life and Beauty itself, but a shimmering curiosity so much deeper, an aliveness that ever expands itself through the interaction of infinite creative beings co-creating together.

I experienced first hand the ways my own life force and consciousness can interact with Nature, communing and communicating with beings beyond the mundane reality like the Star Nations and the Fae Realm.

The Alive and Organic realms of reality didn't have to work hard to find a permanent home in the deepest wells inside my Heart. Lucidness came over me, as I breathed deeply with the perfection of nature and the magic and aliveness that can only be accessed beneath the surface of mundane conscious awareness.

Often times I looked back into my upbringing and the times I spent immersed within the false matrix. I contemplated on the intensity of separation that everyone lived in, oblivious to these other realms of beauty, magic and love. These contemplations broke my heart, but strengthened my Spirit.

The deeper I fell in love with the Beauty of the multidimensional Universe, the more purpose I also felt in my Heart to protect it and the more strength I felt in my resolve to wake humanity up and embody the ways to restore harmony to the Earth.

CHAPTER 8

Sasquatch Rescue

My work in Vermont lasted about 3 months, during which time our household adopted a litter of 4 magical kittens - Jupiter, Maia, Sophia and Hopi. They were 5 weeks old when they arrived, barely walking. By the time they were 6 weeks old, they were connected to their galactic teams and fully functional galactic energy workers!

How miraculous and brilliant these little creatures were. Some of my favourite moments were sleeping with all of them on top of me in my healing room which had enormous windows which faced my beloved mountain.

Once the kittens were all walking and running, I noticed that one of them was always following me around the house. Jupiter constantly followed me and meowed at me with his tiny kitten body. When I held him up to my chest and put his face up to mine, there was a whomping telepathic communication channel between us.

I would ask him, "Are you my familiar?" He would meow. I would ask him, "Are you coming on my adventures with me?" He would raise his hand and meow. Any time I called his name he came running. I started to train the kittens to go in the car with me when I went to the grocery store.

One night I had worked on a particularly difficult client who had satanic abuse experiences. I was very tired after our session and forgot to smudge before falling asleep. Very quickly I entered into a very dark nightmare. I rarely ever have nightmares, and this one was very interesting. It took place in the same room my physical body was in - a very malevolent energy was floating around the house.

I woke up briefly to the sound of tiny meows, Jupiter and Hopi the boys were right on top of my chest smacking my nose with their tiny paws and meowing incessantly. Sophia and Maia were standing on my belly looking over the boys also meowing. I thought: "how strange! Hey cats, what's going on?"

Before I knew it, I was asleep again and back inside the same satanic nightmare. I walked into the kitchen in my nightmare and a demon was there waiting for me.

Again I woke up to the sound of tiny meows, Jupiter and Hopi are still on top of my chest smacking my nose with their tiny paws, though this time Jupiter was looking a little annoyed, like "for real Mom, really? You fell asleep again? C'mon…"

I was between dream and waking reality. I looked up and could see a dark cloud hanging in the air in my room. I looked up at Jupiter and said: "what's going on Ju? What's that all about?"

He looked at me as if I'm a novice and he a grand master and said, "Mom, you left a mushroom tea on your altar for 3 days it grew mould. The spirit of the tea and the mould gave rise to this entity that's messing with you right now!"

I said to him: "Wow Ju, thank you! What do I do?"

He says, "Well, you take the cup with the mouldy tea, pour it down the sink, and rinse the cup of course!"

For some reason my body was limp, I guess still paralyzed from being half asleep. I didn't gather enough wakefulness to follow up with his advice. I ended up falling back asleep, right back into the same nightmare. It didn't take long before I woke up again to tiny paws hitting my nose and little high pitched meows…

Jupiter was looking annoyed as ever like, "C'mon Mom are you serious! Wake up!" I looked up at my kittens, thought to myself, what reality am I in..? I grumbled a little and got up to take my possessed tea to the kitchen.

It was morning already and the dawning sun was peeking through the windows. I rinsed the cup out with water and soap and returned to my bed and kittens. The nightmare was gone.

~ ✺ ~

My work in Vermont lasted a little over 3 months and soon enough I heard the Earth whisper again that a new adventure was beckoning. Just as spontaneously as the ceremonies would gather, the work with the Pleiadians at this coordinate was complete and the energy dispersed. Within a week or two people moved out, the house went on the market, and I ended up with 4 kittens living with me in my car.

By this time it was the beginning of July. Summer was slowly crawling in and it was a good time for an off-road adventure. I felt the wind calling me to go West, and so I just started driving with my pack of cosmic kitties in tow.

At first I didn't know where to go. I decided that maybe I will return to my sanctuary in New Mexico for a quick re-grouping. After a day and a half on the road of marathon driving towards New Mexico, I realized I was going the wrong way. Something just felt off. I just wasn't going the right way.

Now it's important to note that it didn't really matter to me where I was going, because I was plenty occupied just driving. There was so much energy to clear and so many tangled up leylines to restore, it really didn't matter where I was at all.

The biggest energy I was clearing was that of human trafficking. I was very aware intuitively of the fact that I was tracing certain routes where humans were trafficked in plain sight. This intensely traumatizing energy was being imprinted into the leylines and it was apart of the mass consciousness control system.

I realized that my own spontaneous, completely sovereign nature of how I was living my life was itself a part of the Freedom codes that was anchoring into the leylines, dissolving the reversal energies in the grid and providing the nourishment and antidote. It's not enough to just be aware. We have to embody the medicine.

That day I connected with a grid-work sound healer friend of mine, Sarah, who lives in Portland, Oregon. She informed me about some grid-work we had to do together. I literally swerved my car away from going south-west, to going north-west towards Portland. Good thing I was only in Missouri.

The third day of my cross continental pilgrimage was July 6, my birthday. I woke up this morning parked in a truck rest-stop at the side of the high-way, feeling free and wonderful. The kittens were up and meowing for their breakfast. I thought to myself: Xi, you are 24 years old today… what the heck are you doing?

Yes. Waking up on the side of a high-way in a small silver VW Jetta with 4 kittens as co-pilots on a mission with "aliens" to "liberate the collective consciousness of Earth" is indeed what I was doing. In light of this strangeness I decided to dedicate my birthday to a simple meditation. My Life's Purpose.

Why was I born on this planet 24 years ago on this day? I prayed silently as I drove, and I asked for Great Spirit to send me any signs which would give me clarity and resolve on my journey.

I was in Kansas City; it was 3:33 PM. My phone begins blaring an incessant alarm that I'd never heard before. The first thing I noticed when I picked it up was the fact that it was 3:33 PM. I tried clicking buttons to shut the strange alarm off but couldn't and as I took a closer look at the screen, it read: "Amber Alert, Child Missing."

My heart sank. I asked the Great Spirit for a sign about the Purpose of my Life on this day that I was born. And at 3:33pm, I find this blaring message. By this point of the drive, I had already followed a truck which I felt had terrified children energy inside of it and cleared several trains of the same energy. My mind was clear and my heart was full of resolve - I am here for the Children.

The Children doesn't necessarily mean only humans of young age. I feel that standing up for the Children also meant creating safe and healing spaces for the fragmented, oppressed and scared inner children inside all people, recognizing their aliveness and existence and authentic expression of creativity.

The rest of the drive was quiet, swift and easy. My prayers had been answered and I felt joyful and happy with myself to know that I am a young person who is dedicated to Truth and Guardianship of Innocence and Magic.

When I arrived at my friends house in Portland in the afternoon of the next day, I was extremely relieved to say the least. And the kittens were happy to finally be out of the car.

~ ❀ ~

The peace and joy of arriving stayed only for the evening, as the mysterious call started up again. In the middle of the night I started to hear screaming. At first it sounded like children, then soon also women. When I went outside to get a closer ear, I realized that the sound was coming from a different dimension!

The screaming continued for an hour or two and finally ceased at some point and I went to bed. The next evening around midnight, it started again. I went outside once more to realize that the sound was not coming from any house, but a different dimension. They sounded like memories or a frozen moment in time-space.

The next day I asked my friend about the incessant screaming. Even though she didn't hear it, she told me that some weird things have happened around here. That a couple years ago her neighbors were arrested for having a meth lab in the basement, and back in those days there was human sex trafficking that happened in that basement too.

That afternoon I mustered up my courage and divine protection and called on my very psychically gifted friends Barbara Buck and Nichole. We met up in the astral and also connected via Zoom. We put on our various astral invisibility cloaks and went on a little psychic recon mission together.

The first thing we saw via psychic sight was a large, black portal. The portal had black lines going out in many directions, like highways of energy. These lines connected other portals all over predominantly North America but many went all over the world.

The coolest thing about going on astral missions with your friends is that we all report on seeing the same thing! It's quite an incredible feeling to have confirmation on astral sight. Undoubtedly, with each thing that we speak we become more and more confident of our shared experience.

Guarding the portal was 4 very large insect-humanoid looking beings, I felt like they were managers as their energy was that of being in charge. They each had some sort of energy weapon that resembled a machine gun. Apart from those 4 large beings, smaller entities came and 'drank' from the portal, which felt like a cesspool of nasty energy. It was apparent that these bigger beings were running a business, like some sort of loosh restaurant.

Before continuing on, we cross-referenced again what we were seeing, and Nichole made sure our invisibility cloak was on right. We checked in with each other and decided to investigate further.

We sent our psychic awareness through the portal and directly below it several hundred feet was a giant black cube. It looked like some sort of external hard-drive. Upon closer inspection, it was a technology which hosts and duplicates mass viral implantation through pornography. Held inside this drive was energetic information of millions of people that had watched a specific frequency of porn. It harvested their distorted sexual energies.

As if we all had the same hunch at the same time, I blurted out: "I know we all wanted to destroy it at first, but then I think if we went any closer the cube is going to disintegrate into a million tiny AI spider bots."

Barbara and Nichole responded that they both felt the same, and that we needed to have some sort of game plan in order to deal with this thing. We decided that one of us would create a very strong vacuum for when the AI spiders dispersed, one of us would reclaim the information and energy and return it to their rightful owners, and one of us would stay alert for any possible altercations.

I think when we get into this sort of cinematic situation in the astral plane, it's almost like a video game that pans out. It's a visual and symbolic way for our human brains to process the collective healing work we do. We took care of that astral cube that day, but the sexual degradation and deviance viruses in the larger collective consciousness take much longer to clear.

When the black cube was cleared out, Barbara and Nichole both had to go. I thanked them for their support, we were happy for a job well done. I knew that my mission here was not totally over yet.

I went into the living room of the house where I was staying and found that Sarah was playing her cello. I informed her that I was going to do a little grid-work on the portal systems around her house, and lay down on the couch to continue my astral adventure to the sweet sound of her cello.

It didn't take me long to get back into that realm. I ensured that I was well cloaked as I approached the portal. Then something wild took over me, and almost like flushing a toilet I began to grab those guard entities by the scruff and tossing them into a source light recycling machine. The black goo of nastiness began to slowly transmute, as fragments of lost and tormented spirits are freed.

I opened up a connection to a healing realm for those spirits, mostly children, and was so grateful to witness a moment of divine grace and relief for them. As the portal system cleared, large chunks of black yucky stuff started to clear, transform, and restore to colours like green and blue.

Then out of nowhere to my total surprise, these two giant Sasquatch beings jumped out of the portal! They were at least 8 feet tall and they were standing in front of me. Their bodies were made of mostly light but I could see their face and body structure.

Without moving their mouth using what I assume is telepathy, I started to hear one speak. "Hey Sister! Thanks for that! We were trapped in there for quite a while... The interdimensional portal system was once a thriving highway for multidimensional and mystical beings of the Earth to transport long distances across the planet. Since the astral got taken over and polluted by unloving beings, many portals were taken over, clogged up and turned into reversal feeding grounds. Many of these portals are sites where ritual abuse occur and these satanic practices are what sustains the reversal grid."

They blasted me with a wave of expansive enlivening energies as if to say, "Thank you, until we meet again!" and disappeared.

The next day I sealed up the cleared out portal with a Lemurian quartz crystal to assist in the healing of that part of Earth's energy system. When I threw the large crystal into the thick grass where I felt was the epicentre of the portal, I felt like the crystal fell through a long, long tunnel taking light-codes along with it.

CHAPTER 9

Stargate SG-1 & the Astral Military

By now it was early August. I was in touch with Kevone and Michelle who had appeared in my dream in the beginning of this year of 2018. They were my mission support while I was on the road. Their knowledge of the human design system allowed me to feel less strange and abnormal, more empowered in my individual soul path.

When my mission was over in Portland, I was invited to visit them in Colorado Springs. Kevone informed me that their backyard looks unto the legendary Cheyenne Mountain, made famous by the Stargate movie and TV series which divulges a secret Stargate that was controlled by some level of secret military.

The mystery of a folks-tale Stargate was hard for me to pass up, and I got on my way almost immediately. And if you're wondering about those kittens, they all found their own forever homes with starseeds in Washington state. Of course Jupiter found his belonging with me, and the two of us went on our way towards Colorado!

Driving towards Colorado was very interesting, the energy was very different from Oregon. In many ways there are ascending matrices in both states, yet they have very different shadow aspects. In the case of Colorado, it is a heavy infiltration of Military energy due to the presence of NORAD, the USAF, and one of the largest underground bases on this continent.

First entering their house, I felt a certain magical quality to the space. It felt like the house was much bigger than it looked like from the outside. The first night I arrived, Michelle and Kevone had to drive their family to the airport and I was left alone in the house.

It felt like some sort of initiation to the space because when they left, time started dilating and as well as the walls of the house. They have two beautiful Papillons named Yoshi and Lucien. Yoshi the black and white 7 month old puppy was very adamant about playing with Jupiter, my 5 month old wizard kitty. Jupiter didn't like it, he was running away from the incessant chasing games for 3 hours.

Being alone in this new magical home with 3 charmed animals yet very tired from my long journey here, I decided to meditate inside one of the copper pyramids in the house.

Suddenly Yoshi came running out of a room yelping in pain. I assumed that Jupiter had finally had enough of Yoshi's games and maybe smacked him in the face. I ran after Yoshi and made sure he wasn't hurt. He calmed down and seemed to return to normal, so I went back to my meditation.

Within 30 minutes, the house became eerily quiet... too quiet... Lucien the older dog was lying beside me in the copper pyramid. He stood up as I did and noticed something odd too. I went downstairs and Jupiter was looking at me very strangely.

"Yoshi!" I called out. I looked outside, in every room upstairs and down, and realized that he had literally vanished!

When I realized Yoshi had vanished, Lucien suddenly vanished too. I spent the next hour looking inside every room, closet and bathroom, under every bed, behind every sofa... I looked everywhere at least 3 times but the dogs were gone.

At this point a crazy downpour started; lightning and thunder and a very thick heavy rain rolled in. Jupiter was acting very strange. I decided I would have to go back into meditation and try remote viewing in order to find them. I went into meditation and began to call out for the dogs. After a while, I heard the tinkering of a dog's collar.

I jumped up and down the stairs, still no dog in sight! I was then guided to open the back yard door... and there was Yoshi... drenched and shivering. I wrapped him up in a lush towel and was guided upstairs, where I opened the door to the bedroom and there was Lucien, the other dog!

I warmed up and dried off Yoshi, the poor puppy was soaked and freezing. By this time he was clearly a little scared of Jupiter, he was over the chasing game and left him alone! It appeared as if Lucien was very upset with Jupiter, and Jupiter waltzed around still a little strange but obviously sly with himself...

I deducted that Jupiter sent Yoshi outside through a portal, then Lucien astral projected out to find him... It's the only logical explanation after literally looking everywhere for an hour. They were not in the house!

Soon after that Michelle and Kevone came home. I told them what had happened and that it felt like quite the welcome from the enchanted house! They were fascinated by my story yet not totally surprised. I guess stories like these come with ascending into and embodying higher dimensions of consciousness and living beside an underground military base potentially housing a stargate!

In all honesty when I arrived there I had no idea what a stargate was. I'd read about them and heard about them from gatekeepers and channelers, but I had no practical experience with them myself. I also knew that I was about to get a whole education on this subject and was very excited.

The first few days sleeping in my new guest room I had many dreams of this mountain, including seeing its geometric form of triangles and light. I was mapping out the energetic signature of the mountain for the work that lay ahead.

Kevone and Michelle both study and work with the Human Design astrology system intimately, and a big part of being with them was feeling how spacious and peaceful life can be if everyone is aware of and in respect of each other's unique and individual energetic traits.

So the first month I was there, it felt so much like a soul vacation. To finally be in a place where I can have my own private space, and be with people that totally understood, respected and even encouraged my alone time. A place where people truly understood just how important it was for me to be in absolute peace! This first month felt so good to us, and there was still gridwork to be done. I ended up staying for another few months.

After the first month of predominantly rest and recuperation from the previous few months of ardent traveling, new frequencies of psychic lightwork started coming through.

~ ❄ ~

This next part I am about to describe to you will be harder to articulate than anything I have shared with you so far. The best way I can begin is by saying that after developing my psychic sight and healing capabilities for a couple of years rather intensively, a far more complex skill of psionic redaction emerged.

One day I took a wrong turn off the highway coming home from the grocery store. Actually, a more accurate description would be that a force beyond my conscious mind took control of my hands and turned the wheel to take the exit towards the Cheyenne mountain military base.

When I realized I had taken this turn I was already halfway off the ramp, which pretty much lead immediately to a big guarded gate. A few meters before meeting the guards was an opportunity to u-turn back towards the highway. Of course I took the opportunity, but in a mystical state of mind I drove around in a circle a couple of times before driving back out towards the highway. While I was looping around outside of the gate, I felt a piece of my self fly into the base.

This experience was strange but I didn't think much of it, I figured I had gone there to exchange some codes with the mountain and appease my soul's curiosity of what's actually down there.

That evening after nightfall sitting in my room with my cat, the space inside my room started to shift. The air became wavy and other dimensional energies and light opened up. I sat in meditation preparing for my mission. Soon enough I connected with that aspect of me inside the military base.

I felt my guides say, "In and out! We are not here for a tour." My consciousness went right to a space where I felt some sort of technology which utilitzes frequency to alter and contain brainwaves of common civilians, also known as mind control. I also felt the presence of several unkind interdimensional beings I was assigned to transfer.

I felt several of my allies come in, we opened a source-light recycling portal and began to process dark energies through it. The entities went through first, they were easy to take care of. What was more fascinating was the complexity of the mind control systems. I could tell this was going to take more than one night's work and decided to take a good look.

What I learned that night was the unity of consciousness. There truly is no separation, and the false belief or idea that our minds and bodies are separate from each other is indeed a part of the mind control. It keeps humanity from allowing their own consciousness to sink into the collective unconscious that we are all connected to, like a collective neural-network. This also separates our consciousness with other frequencies of consciousness where divinity and mysticism live. The individual consciousness is confined inside a separation prison, with their own disbeliefs forming the bars.

This collective consciousness highway neural-net is what allows me to journey inside of it to release, restore, and recode using psionic redaction. I teach this in my grid-work classes because I think this is a different dimension of grid-work pertaining to our consciousness, not only the physical leylines of the Earth. Of course the energy of the earth directly affects our human consciousness and vice versa and doing these two different frequencies of grid-work will accelerate the other in a complementary fashion.

Through my excavation of the collective unconscious and the mind control systems hidden there, my work became clear for the following months living in Colorado Springs. I was content to call it a night so I cleared any trace of my presence, returned that piece back to my body, and closed the portal.

~ ❀ ~

The missions came often. Usually in the night. There's something about spirit journeying at night that makes it much easier, perhaps because more people are asleep and the consciousness pathways are cleaner. One night as I was sitting on my porch, I started hearing a strange melody. As if playing out of a children's toy piano, the melody was a simple loop. It created a strange resonance of aloofness in my mind, and when I grounded into my body a little, I realized I was hearing the sound via clairaudience.

I went back inside my energy body and was already preparing for another night's mission. Sitting on my bed, I closed my eyes to enter my spirit journey, following the faint trail of the toy piano song. Soon I found my awareness inside artificial realities, swirling in and out of each other. These artificial realities in time-space were created by cartoons and video games.

The main cartoon that came forth to be recoded that night was this Japanese anime called Sailor Moon. Embedded within the frequency of expression and voices of the show were subconscious programs of pedophilia and sexual perversion. These frequencies interact with our subconscious mind which is extremely connected to our energy body, inviting the installation of implants.

This experience helped me learn the ways energy and unconscious thought programs can travel person-to-person via the collective consciousness neuro-net. So even if the voice actor was saying something completely benign and they themselves had no conscious idea they were transmitting distortion codes, if they grew up in a world or culture which normalizes sexual perversion, these energies are embedded in the geometry of the sound they express. Imagine this same concept applied to an actor who has participated in satanic abuse rituals...

One can easily see how popular media and hollywood uses the multidimensional reality of the collective consciousness neural-net to disseminate mind control on the masses. Once the false reality belief systems infiltrate every level of society, it simply perpetuates itself with the older generation grooming the next.

Coming back to exploring how cartoons and certain video games affect our mind, I have long noticed that soul retrieval practices are transforming due to recent drastic changes to our intimate relationship with technology. Most fragmentation of the soul happens during extreme moments of trauma or boredom when the soul splinters and parts escape or leave to other dimensions. I've been finding fragmented mind pieces in artificial realms due to video games.

The insidious thing about these artificial realms is that they are created in the false matrix frequency, embedded full of violence, and sexual and intellectual degradation, trapping parts of our mind inside that frequency reality.

This made me think of my 14 year old brother who still lives with my parents in Ontario, Canada. He spent many hours a day deep inside video games and youtube videos. When I visited them over family vacation time, I always saw him watching extremely dark and twisted videos on youtube, most of them having millions of views, by predominantly children under 15.

I won't go into the specific correlations between these popular videos and games and pizzagate. To me it feels like these videos are grooming young children to normalize satanic ritual violence and demonic frequencies. There were even viral sensations of scary looking entities encouraging young people to commit suicide.

On another night of missioning, I tracked and found a reptilian ship which was influencing certain humans to create some of these videos. Their intention was indeed to hook into human consciousness and create pathways for demonic possession and parasitism.

Despite all of this mission work happening many nights a week, I enjoyed a magical life of beauty and joy, visiting the hot-springs and making music on my days off. Aside from all the astral military weirdness, Colorado Springs was a super pleasant place to be for a while.

~ ❀ ~

I am going to back up now and step away from the ultra disturbing reality that still exist in certain places on Earth, lots of places actually. It was never my 'dream' to dive head first into the most lucid multidimensional perspective on the mind controlled muggle world. It was my dream to be of service to humanity, to become absolutely lucid walking through this reality. This one simple intention was the light which lead me.

All events naturally unfolded over many years of devoted self work, sharpening my psychic abilities, and intending to know the Truth and following my Purpose no matter what. None of this is glamorous and sometimes it's gnarly the places we travel to in order to bring our light and coherence.

Halfway through my stay in Colorado I received another invitation to partake in an Ayahuasca ceremony in Boulder. I again went through the same resistance as I had the first time this year and in the end agreed to go due to feeling guided to be there.

The medicine this time was really gentle, and I was doing breathwork and staying on my pallet. I cloaked my energy field and what I was doing from others, especially the medicine man. I already knew this journey was mission related, and in all honesty, most medicine people have no clue about the astral military. It wasn't their job to know it, it wasn't their job to deal with them.

As the medicine came on, I started to travel into a realm of consciousness where the control systems originated. I happened quite some time ago, yet not as long as they want us to think.

The frame doorway of the house had a massive wooden T-frame with a triangular set of windows above it. In my ayahuasca visions I continuously watched the top of this cross looking beam turn into an oval as in the ankh, and back to a line like the cross. All the while I was receiving the knowing that our infinite, multidimensional consciousness had been hijacked through programmed religions, symbolized by the Ankh transforming into the Cross.

I felt the consciousness of the astral higher dimensional beings who crafted this plan of overtaking planet Earth and enslaving humanity. A plan which unfolded over centuries and centuries of forced trauma, mind control and poison. This couldn't possibly have been designed by a human family - it was the work of beings beyond the 3D, casting a blinding spell over humanity.

I saw this force which I felt inspired to call the Astral Military, creating false religions like catholic christianity, which became open portals for evil beings to infiltrate and control human society. This force distorted ancient spiritual understandings like the Ankh to take away multidimensional perception and understanding from humanity which makes them easier to control.

The interdimensional control system of Earth and Humanity is indeed a spiritual construct. Their ownership of occult spiritual knowledge and deleting it from human awareness was what allowed them to have such incredible control over humanity.

At some point at the peak of my medicine experience sitting in lotus position, I experienced the insides of my body as an infinitely expansive sky of stars. A deep sense of joy, peace, love and magic permeated my entire body and consciousness which are completely one thing. There were no more constrictions, knots, soreness or darkness anywhere. I could feel my cells joyfully communicating with each other.

It was a deeply profound moment because I've had a lot of very difficult ayahuasca sittings, bent over the bucket processing generations of agony and fear. In that moment I realized that this state of Clarity, Expansiveness and Joy was how we were designed to enjoy our human experience all the time. Never were we meant to forget our Self and live out of alignment with our self, leading to dis-ease, malfunction and pain in our body and consciousness.

For hours until I grew tired and fell asleep, I basked in this delightful experience of complete body-energy-consciousness integration with the Divine. I felt deeply that this was supposed to be the baseline experience of all human beings. I felt that the normalization of disconnection and dysfunction was a product of systematic societal mind control.

Waking up to this, we realize that our individual return to this state of complete integration and divine oneness in body-energy-consciousness through self healing and spiritual practices is the only thing which matters in the grand scheme of things. We cannot change the frequency of the reality without healing the distortions and density within ourselves.

~ ❁ ~

CHAPTER 10

Titicaca, Tiwanaku & Ancient Creation Magic

Living high up in the Andean Mountains of Peru was a dream of mine. Ever since connecting with Ayahuasca, I have wanted to visit her home. With December rolling in quickly, along with the snow and the disappearance of the Sun, I made an effortless decision to rent a small house up the mountain in Coya, Peru for a few months to bypass the winter.

Filled to the brim with idealism, we journeyed to Peru, Jupiter in tow. Arriving in the mountains was nothing short of magic. The expansive aliveness of the mountain swallowed me whole in awe of the majesty of this beautiful planet we inhabit. My child-like idealism didn't last long before I began to notice the devastation of colonialism in the local cultures.

As much as I'd loved to go to parties and sound healing ceremonies in the ayahuasca town of Pisac, I could never really jive with the frequency of people there, because I felt like there was something unspoken. I didn't know how to bypass the difficult feelings of anger and disgust with what had happened here. The missionary church stood tall and proud in the centre of the town, and when the pastor passed by everyone lowered their heads to say: "hello father." I didn't find anything to celebrate about inside this.

Posters on cafe walls advertised ayahuasca and other indigenous plant medicine ceremonies to tourists. Travellers from all over the world came here to find some sort of spiritual growth, yet are deceived by money-motivated locals who felt they deserved to sell fake medicine to foreigners for what they'd done to their culture. All a very dangerous mess.

Sometime after living in our mountain adobe home, a very sick man was invited to visit our property by my land-lady who is a local healer. When this super sickly skinny caucasion man arrived at our house, with visible ulcerations and a pale face, I was deeply concerned for his life.

He shared with us stories of his treks into the jungle to study with men who claimed to be medicine men, but turn out to be sorcerers who cursed him with andean magic just for being white. They were angry with the white people who conquered their land and people, and they were taking it out on ignorant spiritual seekers who didn't know any better.

Needless to say the idealism with which I arrived in this sacred country dissipated rather quickly, and my heart ached with the land which ached for the love of its people.

About a month into my stay in Peru, I met a woman named Lisa. When we first met, we were with a group of women my landlord introduced me to. She dragged me to this "goddess full moon meeting", fully knowing I am gravely allergic to superficial spirituality embedded within colonized consciousness. I couldn't stand to be hanging out with "supermodel goddesses" with lots of money from their false matrix successes, who spend it buying other culture's spirituality which their ancestors destroyed.

Yet when I saw Lisa, I realized that she's the reason I showed up at this boring gathering. Barely surviving the sharp knives of subconscious competitiveness and passive aggression, I saw her giggling like a little girl. Ah yes, a spark of life inside her.

I bumped into her again a week later at the market, where she was ecstatic to see me! She exclaimed: "I've been thinking about you for a week! I feel so strongly that I am being called to Bolivia to visit Lake Titicaca and the Tiwanaku Ruins soon, and when I think about this I keep seeing you. I feel like we are supposed to go there together."

I didn't have to think twice about this one and immediately replied: "Yes! I've been thinking of going there as well, and I would love to go there with you!" Within a week's time, the route was plotted and bus tickets were purchased. Lisa and I were embarking on a new adventure to Bolivia.

That same day I was walking down the street when I saw a mural artist painting a street corner. Something stopped me to watch her for a little while. She was painting over the previous mural with a beige paint, clearly painting on the nose of a lion. Something made me remember this specific scene, as if it was significant somehow.

~ ❀ ~

I gave Lisa plenty of preparatory notifications that travelling with me is both exciting and unpredictable. I told her that since I've been listening and walking closely with the Earth and Spirit for many years, we make sudden twists and turns together without obvious indications. At this point, my telepathic guidance system was strong and robust, and as a Splenic Manfestor in the human design system, my now-moment decision making authority, the Spleen, was fine tuned.

I told her that we are likely not on a tourist romp around the ancient ruins, but in actuality on a gridwork mission.

The first stop we made was at Lake Titicaca, in a Bolivia-Peru border city called Copacabana. We were recommended a particular hostel which had incredible clay architecture, created by a famous sculptor from Germany. The houses were all shaped into spiraling seashells and other beautiful structures.

Sitting inside this spiral seashell house, windows overlooking the immaculate sunset moving across Lake Titicaca was one of the most serene and beautiful moments of my entire life. The water lit up a mystical pink and purple matching the sky, as portals spun gracefully into the underwater worlds of the inner-lake…

I heard that this lake is akin to the womb of the world, both from the natives storytellers, and the studies of geomancy which often referred to Lake Titicaca as the Sacral chakra of the world. The indigenous told tales of this lake being "the centre of the world, where all of Life began." This mades sense, as the sacral chakra is the womb. I felt that perhaps all souls, creations and timelines enter and are gestated here in this power centre of the world.

Gestation takes place here, and many starseeds incarnate through this portal and leave pieces of themselves here to be retrieved at a later time upon awakening. I certainly felt the specialness of this lake as I embraced her, feeling as if we are at the centre of the universe.

This lead me into countless hours of contemplation about the state of the world and our creativity. The state of humanity's sacral chakra, the degradation and enslavement we have experienced, and how this could be reflected in the macrocosmic scale of the living planet.

My galactics informed me that this is indeed a continuation of the work we were doing together in Vermont a year prior. We are weaving the pleiadian timeline technology in through the lake to activate its power to support lightworkers to jump planetary realities!

They showed me this in the form of mandela effects. They showed me that when lightworkers fully awaken to our power as creator beings, and work synchronously across the globe, we create these portals which look like tall streams of light, which pull all of humanity through to higher realities. We notice the shifts in mandela effects, but this is operational and intentional.

Imagine that in one reality, a person might be an AI infested, illuminati controlled clone. With the support of this reality jumping light technology, we can jump all of humanity into a reality where this same person might actually be a starseed or awaken to a healing journey which catalyzes major planetary shift from the ground up. This is only one small example.

As I moved into meditation, I received a mandate. This mandate was being coded into the light technology weaving into the womb portal of our mother planet, as if we are shooting a vaccine and system upgrade into the collective consciousness:

- Total sovereignty of life upon earth in all dimensions
- Total obliteration of child & sex trafficking
- Total obliteration of transhumanism timeline
- Total obliteration of slavery, domination & control
- Total apocalypse of all hidden information from humanity
- Total lucidity for all of humanity

When I came out of this reverent commune with the lake, Lisa and I went to soak in the hot tub as the sun was setting. I felt the presence of innumerable light ships giggling and swishing in the sky, playing with the light of our consciousness. Then a parade came through and musicians were singing… people put flowers all over the property… it turned out that we had arrived on the day of Festival of the Goddess.

~ ❀ ~

Lisa and I weren't sure if we would stay here for one or two nights, so we only booked the room for one. When the morning came, my Spleen received directions from Spirit, and we were to leave the hostel immediately! I informed Lisa that in order to stay in the stream of synchronicity we have to get on the road as soon as possible. I told her that instead of taking the tourist busses we will travel with the locals.

At first she was reluctant, but when I told her that if she was not coming with me right in this instant, that I would still have to go right now, she hurriedly came along. I told her that this energy of haste coming through me wasn't actually me, but the Great Spirit. I never know why I have to be places at certain times, but I don't question it. There are bigger parts of me that know way better than the little me inside my brain. When Spirit says Go, I go.

We followed a hand-drawn map provided by the hostel to a local square in Copacabana where busses left for other cities. The bus ride was 3 hours to the Bolivian capital of La Paz, swirling around the mountain sides and chasing the edges of the lake. The country scenery of Bolivia took my breath away and every moment I was so grateful to be alive in this body, to experience this grace.

At some point we had to come off the bus and cross a body of water on a raft, while the bus itself crossed on a much larger raft. We walked to the pier and saw tens of street merchants selling fried trout and potatoes. The energy of Bolivia was smooth, kind and mystical.

Compared to the new age ayahuasca tourism town of Pisac, what I'm sensing in Bolivia is the same ancestral magic, yet sincere authentic love. There was a deep humility and happiness still in the heart of the locals. As if the virus of colonization hadn't distorted their spirit as much.

Soon enough we arrived in La Paz and decided to take a taxi to the Ruins. It took us a while to find a car that would take us the 1.5 hour trek, but soon we were on our way.

It was almost night time, and I was so excited in the car I could hardly contain myself. Just as we were driving up to the gates of Tiwanaku, a giant green and purple comet ripped across the sky! It rolled across the entire sky for over 10 seconds and our jaws were on the floor. Arriving precisely at the right moment. Like a wizard does.

Already dark, now all we hoped for was a vacancy in one of the local inns. After communing with the locals, our driver took us over to a large hotel. When concierge came out, both Lisa and I thought he was a mythical creature right out of the movies.

The next morning a small white dog found me familiar and lead our way to the ruins. When we started towards the ancient rocks, a certain feeling overcame me. I felt that I was escorting an important high priestess of these ancient temples back to her home and her remembrance. This being was Lisa.

As I laid my hands on the ancient stones, I was immediately transported through my crown chakra into visions of time, unfurling and undulating. The ancient memories inside the stones took me to a time when the indigenous people of this place held sacred, festive ceremonies of devotion and reverence to Creation.

I looked over at Lisa, her eyes were teary, she was remembering something too. Having arrived in town on the Festival of the Goddess, it felt like the whole country was celebrating her return. She was here to retrieve something that belongs to her, that she once had lost.

Being quite focused on my role as protector and escort of Lisa on this mission, I almost forgot I had a task of my own. The open blue sky was calm and beautiful. When we arrived at the main temple complex called Pumapunku, very quickly thunder clouds rolled in with a spiraling cold wind. This tornado like wind blasted open a vortex inside the giant flat stones of the temple. My awareness flew into this vortex and again was taken outside of time, this time to witness the beautiful ceremonies that once had taken place on these very steps.

What I'm about to share with you next is extremely important. I write these words from my heart that these truths which I have witnessed breaks my heart. Yet in witnessing this beautiful magic that still exists just outside of time, that all of humanity have access to at any moment, this fills my heart back up with hope.

Inside this tunnel of spiraling energy, I could feel my body cold and stiff below me still standing on the steps of the temple. I could no longer open my physical eyes, the energy had taken me somewhere else. Stars were whirling and spiraling all around me, and I felt a great ecstasy and joy.

It was night time, and the sky was a great expansive canvas filled up with brilliant sparkling stars. It was a time of New Moon, and the whole city had gathered here, many traveling from far distances to participate in this evening's celebrations. Gathered are a people awakened to their sacredness, grace, dignity and power in the Web of Life.

The technicians of the sacred, the ceremonialists, the priestesses and shamans, recognized their Divine Duty as Gatekeepers of a Powerful Vortex. One which feeds and nourishes Life upon this beautiful planet. They held an air of beauty, grace, sacredness and reverence as the people basked in the presence of a Holy energy. The energy of

Life. The energy of Creativity. The energy of a clear and activated Sexuality channeled through the whole vessel, into the Heart and Soul, and the Body of the Living Mother Planet.

You see, these were rites of Sacred Sexuality. A concept that is difficult to even conceive through the layers of conditioning, trauma, distortion and degradation of sexuality we as a humanity experience today. But as I go deeper into explaining this vision, it will become clear why and how we ended up here.

I shift my awareness to the top of the temple, where I see Lisa back in time. She was the leading priestess of the Temple, recognized for her other-worldly origins, beauty and Wisdom. Within her heart held the codes for the Magic of Creation. Her body was a clear channel for cosmic energy. As she danced gracefully upon the altar, all could feel the brilliant, scintillating cosmic energy that rained down from the cosmos through her.

In technicolours I witnessed this energy come through her and all the dancers, this is only the beginning of the rite. I saw this temple in the sacral chakra of the Earth, one of the major energy centres of the entire planet. Major leylines spanning the entire planet were pumped full of this brilliant cosmic energy by these beautiful rituals. They gave energy and magic to all the realms of living beings upon the planet. An act of beauty and divine service.

Soon the priests joined the dancers on the altar, full of honour and respect in their heart and soul. It is the greatest honor to serve the living divine mother planet and all her creatures in this way, of arousing, playing and amplifying her energy to Nourish All of Life. The priests join their Sacred Partner upon the altar and both breath and express passionately through their dance and movements of their Devotion, Love and Reverence to All of Divine Creation.

Their love for the Perfect Divine Creation pour in and through each other, and in that love they find an arousing thunder of ecstatic energy amplifying and drawing the cosmic energy down from the sky, and into the Earth. This is the Energy of Creation Magic.

As quickly as the tornado came bringing me these visions, I came tumbling down back into my body. I was cold and shivering and it had started to rain. I sensed a dramatic shift in the energy, from an ecstatic reverie to a looming shadowy nightmare.

I looked around me and saw Lisa in her rain poncho. Her face was white as if she'd also experienced something extraordinary. I was too bewildered to talk to her about what I'd just witnessed, and we both started walking further through the ruins.

When we walked by a certain spot, Lisa began to cry. I felt an intense energy lifting out of the rocks and what I saw then is truly deep, alchemical fuel for my mission.

I dreaded what I might see, but I knew I had to go back into the visions. I took a deep breath, affirmed my soul's divine connection to life, and closed my eyes. I was pulled into the vortex out of time again, yet I arrived into a different reality. At a time when the evil arrived on Earth, and the interdimensional forces began to overtake the Earth's major energy portals.

This force melded into viruses which infected the mind. Viruses like greed, avarice, lust and competition. These viruses were created to degrade the honour and divinity of humans, so they could fulfill the evil's agenda. The evil came from a group of beings who severed themselves from the nourishment of Love and source energy - who then realized that in order to survive, they needed another sort of energy. The most powerful of the reversal energies are perverted sexual energies and absolute terror.

In my vision I witnessed this evil cloud enter the minds and hearts of certain people. Then I saw the peak of this disaster, rituals of terror and sacrifice. The priestess that were once so revered and respected, I witnessed the sacrificial removal of their ovaries by priests possessed by this supernatural power.

I gasped for air and was overtaken with fear and frenzy. The storm clouds danced above me as thunder and rain raged. I felt like I was unable to awaken from a terrifying nightmare. I knew there was more for me to take in. I knew seeing lucidly with my own eyes was what I was here to do.

When the hunger for power and more loosh became even more insatiable for the invisible evil which controlled the men, the women were spared and the new interdimensional controllers of the earth and humanity shifted their likings to children. They realized that the purity and innocence of children produced higher qualities of fear.

These rituals are not human. They were not created by humans to satisfy humans. They were created by interdimensional demons who injected humans with fear, lust and power to do their bidding.

When the stones decided I've had enough, I returned to my body from my frenzied visions. To my surprise the sky had cleared up and now a brilliant blue sky radiated a kindness to us. I didn't say much for the rest of that day as Lisa and I went to visit one last monument before heading back to our hotel.

Sexual energy is the Energy of Creation channeled by and experienced through our 3D vessel. This is the most sacred and powerful of all Energies, as it has the power to Create and Destroy. Humanity is a race of Creator Beings, capable of harnessing and transforming this basic form of Magic into any creation we inspire. Music, paintings, architecture, and stories… Establishing a planetary resonance of peace and joy…

How else to control powerful beings like these than to trick us into believing we are not powerful at all? That we are powerless at the whims of the gods, that we are animals who are only capable of reproduction?

Back at the hostel I got to reflect on planetary energy systems. Through perceiving the reality in different layers, in macrocosm and microcosm, the humans living close to the power centres are direct reflections of the health of the planetary chakras. Looking around, I saw impoverished and disempowered indigenous people living a life of poverty and strife. I saw that their sexual and emotional maturity to live life in accordance to the magic that once lived here was meagre.

None of this was their fault by any means. It's simply the current state of energetics on the planet that we are all participating in co-creating. It's not hard to project our minds into popular culture and see how our relationships with our self, our reality and each other can be severely distorted and dysfunctional.

Back at the sacred Lake Titicaca I danced. I journeyed into the lake and communed with the Mer-people there, and a giant spinning lotus flower lit up the whole lake, as we danced this energy of joy, respect, reverence, reciprocity and peace. We danced the mandate codes into the womb and prayed for this energy to move through the leylines to reach the consciousness of all beings…

We are Remembering the sacred magic we once wielded as Guardians and Gatekeepers of this magnificent planet. And through this remembrance, we heal the fragmentation and trauma we collectively experienced from interdimensional planetary trauma, and regain our empowerment and dignity as a planetary species.

CHAPTER 11.

Ariana: Sexual Misery Programming

I didn't realize just how appropriate it was to have this chapter immediately follow the previous one until I began to write it. This is the way my soul and the living planet planned my education, and looking back upon my journey it has always been a progression towards deeper understanding and lucidity in perceiving the world.

When I returned to my mountain home in Peru from Bolivia, a series of unfortunate events began to occur in and around my home. We had our flights booked and rent paid up until May which was still 2 months away. Yet the flow and magic in my life which moved me began to fade and return to mundanity, letting me know something else was about to call.

One day I received an email from a man named Harlan. He heard me on Lauren Galey's podcast Quantum Conversations and was inviting me to speak at his festival, Portal to the New Earth in Joshua Tree, California. I had actually attended this festival back in 2016, and it was my favorite festival! In his email he conveyed to me that he is also from Andromeda, and that he felt like he had been organizing this festival for me.

The festival was headlined by my favorite musicians in the festival circuit. It was too wonderful of an opportunity to pass up! I meditated on the upcoming timeline and realized I had to make a pit stop in Ottawa, Canada for some reason. Logically, this was not really a "pit stop." Having driven across the continent several times, I knew the Universe wouldn't pass up an opportunity for me to do it again.

Within a few days new flights were arranged. A client of mine in Ottawa invited us to stay in her neighbor Janet's apartment while she was on vacation for nearly 3 weeks. When a new timeline was established, doors opened to let us know we were on the right track.

~ ❁ ~

Hanging out in Janet's apartment was odd. Janet was a screenwriting professor and her apartment was filled to the brim with old press releases and books. Ottawa was still snow-filled and cold in late March, and we were happy to have found a cozy warm apartment to configure our latest mission.

One day it came out of nowhere. The world suddenly morphed into a universe centered around Ariana Grande. Some people might know she is one of the biggest pop musicians, or "Illumidonkey" puppets, on the world stage right now. I had no idea. I did not know who or what she was until those few days when the universe decided that it was time I got to know her.

Everywhere I turned I saw her. On billboards, on YouTube ads, and in random shops on walks. One evening hanging out in the living room, Spotify turned itself on and started blaring her songs. I thought this was all very peculiar so I watched some of her music videos. When I saw she had billions of listens on her songs, I was bewildered. She was singing about nonsense!

Three days into this Ariana madness, I received a call from my old friend Danji whom I lived with in Montreal back in those early years.

I hadn't talked to Danji probably in a couple of years, and when he mentioned that he was actually headed to an Ariana Grande concert that night, the whole world stopped. I raised my fist to the sky and yelled: "Really?!"

The bubbling excitement of a new mission was difficult to resist no matter how ridiculous the mission seemed to me at the time. I could hardly believe my team was sending me to an Ariana Grande concert. Montreal was still a couple of hours drive away, so I got in my car and immediately got on my way.

I listened to her music on Spotify in the car. Having been "out of the matrix" for nearly 7 years I was very out of touch with pop culture and 'famous' people. I was truly taken aback by the things she was singing!

I continued to receive downloads on the mind control technologies at play on mass consciousness through the use of sound and sexual degradation. I recognized profoundly that these tactics were reversal distortions in ancient creation magic...

As a sound healer and sonic oracle, I know very intimately the mystical power of music and vocal transmission. That sound expressed via our voice is truly a transmission of our Creator's thoughts and intentions, engraving geometries of light and manifestation onto the fabric of reality which has profound effects on human consciousness and energy bodies.

Sounds expressed in love and reverence create heaven, and entraine our consciousness and energy bodies to vibration in this frequency in co-creation. Sounds expressed in degradation and lust, which create hell, does the same to our mind and subconscious bodies.

I entered the amphitheater at the precise moment the concert began. As I fumbled my way through the enormous theater past excited teenagers and glitzed-out children, I heard her start her first song endearingly called "An Angel Cried." By the time I found my seat she was onto her second song "God Is A Woman."

I found it peculiar that she started the concert with these two songs which seemingly adhered to certain spiritual ideas. However, that feeling was quickly distinguished as she continued on to sing about sexual and relationship deviance and greed. The angel in me twisted and turned inside my belly as I realized that by her singing God is a Woman, her puppeteers were telling me that they have taken the Feminine Creator and made her their prostitute.

I used my psychic sight to take a deeper look into her energy field. I had many different theories about Ariana since her voice was so beautiful. I thought to have a voice that beautiful, one must be an angel. To my dismay, I recognized that the angelic technology was actually her human body and that there was no soul inside her at all. Whatever intelligence inside of her was using her body as a vessel for evil, and this made me quite upset.

Around the third or fourth song, a giant moon descended down to the center of the stage. The whole stage was a circle with a large space in the middle sort of like a ring. When I looked at the back drop, I suddenly realized that the stage looked quite like a toilet. All jokes aside, it really did look like a toilet. The round stage, shaped like a toilet seat, was a walkway where Ariana and her dancers pranced. The backdrop of the stage was the toilet tank. The giant moon descended down the centre of the toilet, it was truly enormous.

When I saw the giant moon overpowering everything on that stage lit up like a christmas tree, a little voice in my head whispered, "Google the Moon Chain Lineage." The first article which came up was a Lisa Renee article from her Ascension Glossary website. I'm going to put the excerpt here which blew my mind.

> https://ascensionglossary.com/index.php/Moon_Chain
>
> "Moon Chain Beings are soulless beings, like the Greys and Zetas, that have been cloned and hybridized for use by the Annunaki, Drakonians, etc. whom have placed these beings as "workers" on various planets… The Moon chain lineages have been directly involved both karmically and technologically with purposely creating the "Sexual Misery" program in the human race during this dark age.
>
> The sexual misery program is to distort, manipulate and abuse the sexual energies, therefore spiritual energies, in human beings incarnated on this planet.
>
> The Baphomet fields are intricately involved in all deceptions and trickery relating to the Seducer Archetype which promotes the Sexual Misery Programming of the lunar forces or Moon Chain Lineages.
>
> Many of these mind control structures on earth were held in place through magnetic imprints transmitted from the Moon, an artificial satellite. The Orion forces from Saturn have been using the moon as an outpost to transmit Lunar forces to earth. They have used the Moon Chain lineages as workers for this purpose for many millennia.
>
> These Moon lineages have been inherently responsible for the mind control transmitted to the earth to create Gender Separation, Sexual Misery, and Misogyny."

For those of you who don't know, Lisa Renee provides in great detail writings on the negative alien control systems of humanity from a highly metaphysical perspective. Very often on my gridworking journeys I would discover certain gridlines or collective curses, and this little voice would encourage me to Google specific keywords which would lead me to her websites to confirm that which I have organically found on my own.

This is probably one of the most intense cases of such an occurrence. I literally just came to my own conclusion that this dancing singing puppet on stage is either completely soulless or a soul that is really not very nice. Then, to hear this voice telling me to Google something completely random like the "moon chain lineage" and be brought to an article so specific about the voodoo she is doing on stage! It's all too much to be a mere synchronicity.

Please note that I have never studied or read through her work intentionally--only in these cases of being encouraged by my multidimensional team to look up certain keywords. It amazes me every time.

I'd just like to add here too as a side note, that I do not feel that these beings are "clones". In my more recent dream journey inside a high tech ET underground laboratory where illuminati puppets are created, I saw that these beings are more accurately described as engineered biological organisms.

They are created with various composites of human DNA, selected for their desired traits and apparences, but are not replicas of one real person. I suppose if the majority of their coding was based on one person, they this would make them genetically modified clones.

Before I continue, I'd like to put an excerpt of a different Lisa Renee article that is highly related to this subject. I think she is very gifted in articulating such difficult subjects.

I AM STARSEED

https://ascensionglossary.com/index.php/Sexual_Misery

"The Sexual Misery program is to intentionally reverse, distort, manipulate and abuse the sexual energies, therefore abuse the spiritual energies, in human beings incarnated on this planet. It is intended to create people with addiction issues that are easily harvested in Reversal Networks for their sexual energy.

The Archontic Deception Strategy is directly to inflict Sexual Misery, sexual abuse and sexual slavery on this planet, starting as early and young as possible. This means the children of earth are targeted for inflicting Sexual Misery Mind Control programming through a variety of hidden agendas, such as Genital Mutilation, Sexual Scams, and using forms of Emotional Manipulation to get them to submit to non-consensual sexual activity or Seducer Archetype behaviors. Children are not mentally or emotionally equipped to discern what adults true motivations are, and grow up into adults that repeat the same abuse they suffered as children.

...The damage promoted in these centers also resulted in emotional distortions and aberrant accumulated energies in the lower bodily energy centers. This was taken advantage of by the negative aliens to splinter the Soul energies by controlling the sexual energies. By promoting distortions around the sexual act, gender roles and corrupting our relationship to our mother and father parent, our race descended into sexual misery and in many cases, forms of sexual slavery.

Moon Chain Lunar Histories

This is known as the "sexual misery program" propagated and controlled by the Moon Chain (lunar) lineages of the NAA (Negative Alien Agenda) on the earth. (These are lineages not indigenous to the earth but came through the process of invasion and deception.) These are multiple layers of architecture and mind control that have been artificially created to control, deceive, separate, confuse, torture and steal human beings sexual life force, and it is a violation against the human soul.

At this point of the concert I'm already bewildered. I was surrounded by young girls aged 6-17 focussing intently and even frenetically on this devastating role model clearly exhibiting distorted and deviant sexual behavior. They were mimicking her dance moves but more insidiously, mirroring her degraded vibration and attitude towards sexuality and life. This is the very surface level of mass Satanic reversal Baphomet mind control.

My mind briefly flashed back to the beautiful visions I had in Bolivia, of the incredibly divine and reverent ceremonies celebrating the divine feminine and the power of our divine sexuality. Placed side by side, this concert was an absolute aberration and wake up call to humanity.

This is an extraordinarily difficult passage for me to write from the perspective of a higher dimensional geneticist. In the higher dimensions, sciences like genetics are very sacred as it is the study of the divine creation itself. To be entrusted with such knowledge from the Oneness of Creation is the greatest honor, and to return this honor we wield our knowledge and power to create Beauty and Love with Care and Devotion.

From the perspective of experiencing a deep reverence for Life, to witness the state of sexual and creational degradation on this planet is heartbreaking. Being at the Ariana concert was like standing at the gate of a portal, witnessing the true state of collective consciousness in real time in 3D. It was a real wake up call for me and rocket fuel for my mission to restore these ancient knowings in the hearts of all of humanity.

I think this was the most important thing that my own soul got out of that evening. It's easy to watch conspiracy theory videos about the Illuminati on YouTube and scream and yell that the world is run by pedophiles. But it's an entirely different experience sitting in the ritual pit with the children, whose parents paid hundreds of dollars for them to receive their mind control. The false matrix has crawled deep within them, and it's going to require intelligence, creativity, love and motivation to help them find the light again.

I snapped out of my concerns by the 5th song and I felt the whole stadium "click-in" to my light technology. My team beamed to me that we were ready to party. Through techniques of psionic redaction we crawled through the collective consciousness and prepared to disseminate antiviral codes of true love, respect and reverence for all of life, the balanced and perfect union of the feminine and masculine principles.

The technology felt similar to a holographic insert, except it was a perception distortion field placed in front of the people's eyes and ears which altered the frequency of sonic and informational input. It changed the distorted codes into the correct codes before it hit the subconscious mind of the receivers, blocking the sexual misery mind control frequencies from integrating into the minds of the children in the stadium.

At some points I was guided to envelop the whole stadium in certain frequencies and colours of light. Within minutes of focussing on that frequency, the projections onto the stage would match that colour and frequency of light. Purple and gold colors restructured the distorted codes of royalty. Glitter broke up the stagnant soulless grey-alien energies. No matter what frequency came through, it always appeared on the stage! I was truly bewildered. The team assured me these were confirmations that the light technology was working.

At the peak of this experience I felt as if I was coming in and out of my body, merging with the light technology to reprogram the mind control. When I returned to my body, I looked up at the stage. She had changed into a different costume, which resembled a young farm girl of about 12 years old. She sat on the staircase of a theater set which looked like a farmhouse. It took me a few seconds to fully snap back into my body to realize she was singing in a very suggestive manner, a lustful song about her daddy.

I felt very angry, as the wrath of a mother bear awakens inside my heart to protect my young from a lustful vampire here to contaminate their precious innocence. I beamed my light technology right at her and began to reconstruct her field and her expression, which was pure garbage projecting outwards into the minds of the children. I was surprised by the malleability of reality myself when she suddenly started to sing about Nature and True Love.

Glitter filled up the whole stage as people swayed their cell phone lights around in the air. I heard "good job, we are complete" from my team, as I felt the replacement codes "click" and sink into the collective consciousness. Ariana was on her last song and I was feeling tired but proud, still bewildered by the reality of all the things experienced this night.

~ ❀ ~

Zooming my awareness out of the Earth while sustaining contact with this frequency of planetary sexual violation tuned me into a layer of the astral plane where I saw a harvesting station. Nearly all people were tagged and connected to this energy-harvesting technology, distorted and perverted sexual energies being the greatest source energy of all. Pornography and subconscious subliminal frequencies projected by popular media implanted into human energy bodies and consciousness hooked people up to the harvesting station.

The human energy system is an intricate and powerful network of energy channels and consciousness that is intimately connected to the energy system of the living planet Mother Earth, as well as cosmic energies penetrating All That Is. Our prowess in channeling massive amounts of cosmic energy through our emotions and sexuality is what made us a likable candidate to be preyed upon by beings who lacked this ability.

In the correct morphology of energy, the human body is a multidimensional conduit for cosmic creation energy. We not only express and experience this creativity in the physical through making art, architecture, and music but also multidimensionally through our energy body and consciousness.

This correct morphology is a coherent system of conscious understanding combined with respect for the divinity of sex and all of creation, as well as physical clear channels of energy. Through the correct understanding and expression of the multidimensional creativity of humanity as the creator guardians of this reality, we collectively create heaven on Earth.

In this perspective we can see how through deceiving and distorting humanity's understanding of sex greatly hinders our ability to wield our power as creator beings. We have been tricked into creating a hell.

The mass mind control and sexual distortion programs have created a global societal acceptance of sexual degradation and deviance.

The knowledge of sacred sex and creation has been reduced to a mere fancy workshop. Sadly looking around the world today, most people's energy systems move in reversals feeding the demon realm without them even knowing.

Our sexual energy is meant to circulate through our body, nourishing every organ, system, and blood cell with vital life force energy, empowering our sacred dream creations. The way sex is portrayed in pornography and popular culture is engulfed in pain-pleasure confusion viruses and implants and leaking energy out of the bottom chakra through careless orgasms. This kind of orgasm is pervasive in most of humanity, and leaks our precious life force right out into the demon realm, a tasty feast of energy to perpetuate a degraded reality.

Looking around our world today, the majority of humanity has little understanding of our True power as Divine Sovereign Energetic Creator Beings. In order for us to transform into an ascended civilization of peace and respect, humanity has to become educated once again on the once not so secret mystery school teachings of Energy and Sacred Sexuality. Through this process of activating Individual Energetic Sovereignty we give interdimensional parasites no chance to grow.

The mass mind control and enslavement programs are multidimensional and require an understanding and perception of Soul-Body incarnation science, which is also closely connected to genetics. Genetics is the weaving of light into geometries which project into forms. It's the study of Divine Intent's Creation of Physicality and Living Organisms.

This weaving can include aspects of the physical body, like the color of skin and shape of nose, but can also include other-dimensional aspects like personality and preferences. Even further more, genetics can also hold codes to skills, perception of time-space realities and potential timelines. These more advanced aspects of our genetics have been shut down through centuries of social mind control and collective amnesia.

As the world discovers the truth about planetary elite pedophile rings and Satanic ritual abuse, it becomes increasingly important for us all to recognize how these energies affect everyone personally and where these distortions hide inside our own body and consciousness. Putting the human representatives of the negative alien agenda in jail is only one small aspect of our work here on planet earth. Assisting in the liberation of all people suffering from centuries to millenniums of sexual misery programming and energetic slavery is the real work at hand for most starseeds.

This very realization helps us slow down, ground into our own lower chakras and earthstar chakra, away from the glitz and glamour of certain new age spirituality ideologies. We came to Earth with our divinity, our magic, and our healing abilities intact. Through integration we move out of seeking and awakening into a stable knowingness of our Self and our task at hand.

As an Angelic Starseed, my soul has come in from a higher dimension beyond Time where the original intent and codes of the Creation of this Universe are intact. We are in a collective process on Earth now awakening from an unconscious evolution of biology to a co-creating conscious evolution with this Divine Intent of experiencing physicality.

Placing this vibration next to the reality of Satanic mind control and abuse makes it very clear that the cleaning and restoration of Divine Consciousness from the effects of these mind control systems and creating bridges and modalities of healing for the mass population to do the same is the extraordinary task at hand.

CHAPTER 12.

Beyond Amnesia: Portals to the New Earth

In the beginning of my awakening in early 2013, I had very vivid consistent feelings that I was inside my own "University Education." The aliveness of the world was conscious to me and in this connection I never felt alone or scared, just taken care of and guided. I communicated to this perceivably "external" reality telepathically as if I was talking to myself. An indescribable love fills this connection, it always took me to where I needed to be and what I needed to learn in order to fulfill my Soul's purpose.

I spent many years exploring different kinds of gatherings. My galactic team encouraged me to think of them as "social evolution technologies." I took this to mean that the multi-dimensional organization, content and experience empowered by the intent and energy of its participants had the power to create visceral evolutionary change to our personal and planetary reality. I attended gatherings which ranged from psychedelic raves under the highway, to academic conferences surrounding entheogenic plant medicines, to ET and disclosure conferences, to permaculture education festivals.

I have participated in events where the collective energy was woven tightly and beautifully into prayers of love and beauty. I have also witnessed events where the collective energy was carelessly directed and harvested by negative ETs and humans for personal gain. My job was basically to learn as much as I could about the different multi-dimensional aspects of organizing a gathering, as well as incorporating galactic light technologies for the collective evolution of human consciousness.

In those first semesters of my Magic Reality School, I sent out a request to the universe that I would like to have a Graduation Party. I expressed to the universe that when I am completing this phase of my training and degree, I would like to celebrate with my soul family at a beautiful festival with my favorite musicians playing. I specifically loved the music of Kalya Scintilla and Yaima and listened to these artists all the time, their sonic frequencies nourished my soul.

As much as this chapter is about my magical graduation ceremony, it is also about the multi-dimensionality and responsibility which comes with organizing and directing the energy and attention of massive groups of people. After many years of research in these wide ranges of gatherings, I knew I wanted my "graduation festival" to be a multi-dimensional, cohesive, grounded and safe container for personal and planetary healing, prayer and connection to the Aliveness of the Universe.

When Harlan reached out to me, stating in his email that he felt like he had "organized this festival for me," I knew right away that he had organized my graduation party. I looked at the line-up and of course Kalya Scintilla and Yaima were both headliners.

Portal to the New Earth felt like an opportunity to simultaneously experience a cohesive compilation of everything I've studied in the past 6 years, like writing a thesis, as well as an honouring of all the magic and energies which move through my vessel. Harlan invited me to speak during the opening and closing ceremony, as well as facilitate a transmission and healing ceremony on both days of the weekend.

As the energy of the festival started to build on the first day, the majestic Boulder Gardens of Joshua Tree transformed into a middle-earth fairy-world wonderland. A galactic buzz rippled across the sky, enveloping the festival grounds in a field of activation, love, excitement and psychic protection.

The galactics were celebrating my arrival at my graduation party, but they also informed me that there was work to do. We would never miss such a golden opportunity for planetary work! They compared this upcoming assignment to a thesis paper. I chuckled.

At the opening ceremony I was delightfully joined by Machu and his wide assortment of sound healing tools. Machu is a magician didgeridoo craftsman whose technique on the instruments transports its listeners to other worlds. Harlan had masterfully weaved our ceremonial sound healing together for the festival and I couldn't be any happier!

I expressed to the hundreds of participants present that day that in order to Portal to the New Earth, we each have to Portal into our own New Earth. This way we each become a Portal for all to the New Earth. New Earth is a Vibration and a State of Being. As within so without, as we anchor and embody and stabilize higher frequencies in our moment-to-moment day-to-day lives, we anchor this frequency onto the Earth making it available to all of Humanity.

And so any portal is an opportunity to deeply cleanse and work on ourselves, supported by the love and joy of soul family reunion. It's only through that work that more light and authenticity is able to anchor into our bodies, thus into the planetary reality.

As night time approached, the energy shifted into a mystical playful fairy-world. A deep expansive peace radiated throughout the property as everyone experienced a feeling of homeliness, a deep breath of relief as a longing is finally fulfilled after surviving so long in the false matrix. It was as if the space allowed each unique being's soul to emerge, to play, to explore, to be with soul family. Relief and excitement permeated the collective aura with a majestic magic that transcended time.

In my transmission on the second day, we covered topics like embodying 7D consciousness and awakening and embodying galactic and mystical aspects of self.

We talked about how the act of allowing ourselves to truly be and become the most unique expression of ourself literally heals the fabric of our reality as we become living portals for Authentic Cosmic Life-Force Energy to flow on the Earth.

Saturday evening was a special night, as my favorite musicians were playing and it was the designated "party night" of the festival. At nightfall I went onto the dance floor and found a charmed bee-hive shaped chocolate still in its wrapper. A curious sparkle surrounded this moment in time, and I knew this was a gift to me from the fairies.

I had actually met the alchemist who made these special chocolates earlier in the day and knew that he was a trusted medicine man. I knew that he made several varieties of chocolates, infusing them with different plants like marijuana and magic mushrooms. The only way to find out which chocolate came to find me was to try it, I suppose!

Please note that this chocolate was a very specific shape with very specific markings on it. Because of these unique qualities I was able to identify the maker and source of this medicine. I would otherwise never ingest random ground-scored charmed chocolates from a festival!

Within an hour I was plenty certain that the chocolate was indeed infused with magic mushrooms. The dance floor was transformed into a portal to another realm. Beautiful beings frolicked on the dancefloor in their beautiful costumes, except they weren't costumes at all but clothes which were extensions of their soul expression. I felt like a galactic visitor who by some random curious magic stepped foot into a fairy party.

I watched as a portal opened up above the dancefloor in the night sky, but it was an access point to another time. Here I received the words, "Beyond Amnesia." I recognized the complexity of my transmissions even deeper through witnessing them in real time. As we collectively accessed these magical dimensions of ourselves and danced and celebrated and expressed ourselves in these dimensions, a palpable vortex energy field was created.

This energy field is an access point beyond the confines of false matrix consciousness and any distorted perceptions of time. It allows people to move beyond the false matrix and into an organic field of consciousness where planetary and collective soul memories can be accessed.

As the portal opened and this energy of Remembrance rushed in, all I could do was stare at the glory and majesty of this heavenly creation in a state of awe. What stood before me was not only an energy vortex, but the original template of the Earth and the magic and libraries of multi-dimensional lifeforms she holds.

In my psychedelic trance, Machu approached me with a giant smile on his face. He appeared as an elder wisdom keeper of the mystical forest races. He looked pleased with my work in helping the forest creatures open this portal. A man dressed in middle-earth attire approached me now, and these words like water fell out of my mouth.

"On behalf of all galactic and ET races, I'm sorry for what happened here on Earth. I'm sorry that certain beings and technologies nearly wiped out this magnificent planet of its magic and ancestral knowing of multi-dimensional physicality." I teared up as I said this as my soul truly felt the agony and pain in the near destruction of this incredible beauty that I myself had taken part in creating.

"On behalf of all earthlings, beings of the fairy-realms and inner earth, ho'oponopono." He reached his hand out slowly towards me as if inciting a high five. I reached out my hand to meet his, and we raised our hands together up to the sky. I felt the reconciliation and forgiveness of the organic living realms of Earth radiate through the dimensions, dissolving layers of collective trauma, fear and hatred.

The psychedelic dream was not a fabrication of my imagination, but simply what allowed me to access and experience a reality far more mystical and alive than the familiar mundane one. This aliveness is always present and looking for ways to help us remember our ancient primordial connection to the living Earth. This connection to the mystical aliveness is our natural, original state of being. Moving our awareness Beyond the Amnesia connects us to this aliveness and our sacred memories and knowledge of our race and planet.

Taking this energy and anchoring into the field, the oracular healing ceremony which took place on Sunday was one of the most powerful ceremonies I've ever facilitated to date. Many distorted fields in our body, mind and unconscious still hold misbeliefs and traumas surrounding sovereignty, abundance, relationships and our own mystical power. By allowing potent energies of Organic Aliveness to penetrate our entire being, these distorted fields are gracefully and powerfully restored.

As soon as the darkness came over the land, I noticed some strange energies. It didn't take me long to deduce that somewhere else in the world, probably close by, a satanic ritual was happening. I was being called to hold another ceremony in collective prayer.

Harlan, being the creative mastermind that he is, had already scheduled Machu and I to perform another sound healing ceremony this evening. The people gathered around the altar and Machu and I got into our positions ready for transmission. Something extraordinary happened then, something not even I had been prepared to express.

As people settled into their spots, I met eyes with Machu to initiate the beginning of our ceremony. Machu began to play his didgeridoo and other instruments. I sat in meditation waiting for a commencing energy to arrive in my vessel to begin singing, but this energy never came. This has never happened to me before and I started to feel a tiny pang of nervousness. I waited another minute or two before I finally felt the energy come in and began to sing.

However something was still different than usual. I felt a very scattered energy, one which made it difficult for everyone in the crowd to focus. An energy was present to distract our collective prayers. I realized this ceremony was going to be a little more difficult and complex than others.

Something came over me and I began to speak. "My brothers and sisters. It brings me such joy and peace to see that so many of us have moved through our awakening and initiations to find ourselves at an event such as this one. I have enjoyed a weekend of healing, remembrance, and being at 'home' with you all, and for this I am eternally grateful.

There is an energy present here tonight which is seeking our love and coherence. As you might be noticing, there is a distracting energy present right now. One that is trying to scatter our awareness away from presence, away from focusing our intent with love. I invite us to not only focus on this energy, but to pierce through it to discover what is at the root.

There is something happening right now that is creating this distortion in the collective energy field, and we have been called together to hold space for its transmutation. Many of you may know that this planet has been ravaged by black magic, rituals which include the mutilation, sexual molestation and killing of children and people.

At an event such as this one we intend to grow and heal ourselves in the intent of creating New Earth. But in order to do that, we have to completely become lucid about the foundations on which we are building the new.

We cannot simply party and bask in our enjoyment, excitement and happiness while neglecting certain energies when they arise. In this moment, there is a distortion energy that is causing us to become scattered and not present here. I want you to pierce through this energy with your awareness and lucidity.

Humanity has undergone planetary sexual enslavement, and the very rituals that perpetuate this reality are happening right now. We cannot call ourselves lightworkers and lightbearers if we choose to ignore and suppress this reality. There is a wholeness that comes from embracing the subconscious pain and agony this free-will violation has caused us both individually and collectively."

At this point, the energy was almost too much to bear. My oracle channel was bringing through an intense experience of lucid feeling into subconscious neglected parts of the planetary and individual subconscious pain body. A deep, gut wrenching cry oscillated through my throat and I began to cry through my heart and belly.

The air felt as if it was frozen for a long time. When the crying subsided, I lifted up my body and returned to the collective space of our ceremony. There was a collective groundedness now, as everyone has sunken into our hearts to hold space for the healing of our collective agony - the proper response to a planet under enslavement and black magic.

There was no more avoidance now. The lightworkers were in integration and acceptance, with an expansion of our heart space to envelop all the evil and prepare for its transmutation.

Words can't really explain how proud I was to have been a part of that spontaneous yet deeply intense ceremony. It not only showed me the power of collective prayer, but also showed me just how much I have integrated, learned and embodied over the past 7 years. I truly experienced that night the power of an Oracle of Divine Love anchored in Truth and Compassion for All of Creation.

We realized together during that ceremony that as beautiful as it is to be joyful and celebrative in each moment, to spiritually bypass all that is scary and uncomfortable in the world is not a lasting solution.

To be able to sustain a deep loving peace in our hearts even as we witness the grimmest of realities is true mastery and what allows us to hold space for deep healing and transformation. In this space of unconditional acceptance and grace, we are given a chance to take responsibility for the co-creation of a better world.

I want to personally congratulate and express publically that Harlan Emil is not only a galactic creative genius in the sacred geometry temples he creates, but a man of integrity, dignity and a true servant's heart.

Portal to the New Earth is a galactic ceremony of healing and reconciliation which healed innumerable layers of trauma stored in the Earth and the participants. The festival successfully harnessed the excitement, love, joy and willingness of the service energy of participants intentionally to open a Powerful Portal through time, allowing fascinating energies of remembrance, divinity and magic to be more accessible by all on Earth.

The multitudes of goodness of this gathering would not have transpired if this gathering was at all distorted by certain viruses like fame and fortune. Certainly in being of service we are deserving and worthy of balanced energetic reciprocity. Yet we can easily discern if these viruses of importance and money are woven into the tapestry of creative motivation. We cannot create a Portal to anything if we are creating with the energies of the false matrix viruses.

Having attended countless different kinds of gatherings and conventions, and witnessed multidimensional hijacking, implantation, energy siphoning - as well as incredible beauty, healing, connection and love, I have deducted this truth. The creational organizing team of an event and their intentions, clarity and integrity truly matters in the creation of time-space experiences. This goes for events, as well as societies and cultures.

For this I am honored and grateful to have been invited to participate in one of the most integral, beautiful, magical and powerful gatherings in the world.

~ ✤ ~

Having experienced the depth, multi-dimensionality, intent and transformational power of a truly service-to-other event, I can no longer see any excuse for gatherings to have holes or energy leaks which siphon the energy of the collective psychically and financially, instead of truly empowering us. Especially if these events are marketed to the awakening community and claim to promote love, light and multidimensionality.

I am led to understand deeply that gathering and focussing the attention of large numbers of people is a great shamanic responsibility. One that requires the organizers and speakers to not only understand and perceive energy and multidimensionality to some extent, but embody that which they preach in order to curate a safe and productive experience for all.

The planetary shift will happen as quickly or as slowly as the way-showers and lightworkers truly heal and initiate our mystical life in trust and surrender to create a foundation for a whole new vibration and collective neural-net. The false matrix of fear, lack and control will not disappear for as long as it still thrives inside the mind and systems of those who appear to be teachers and leaders of our communities.

Unhealed aspects, like parts desiring popularity in high school, and programmed distortions, like lack mentality and hyper intellectualism, are the easiest ways lightworkers with good intentions and kind hearts get tricked into co-creating with the illusion.

At a time of intense planetary transmutation and healing, it's not responsible to believe that it's "good enough" to simply "use fancy words like ascension and intend for the best" while still acting from places of fear and wounds.

Intellectual talk about the astral and other military factions without psychic and energetic mastery opens up portals which infect people with certain frequencies of mind control and fear without this being of conscious intent. This is why consciousness elevation and acquiring energetic sovereignty is such an important inner task especially when one takes up the task of becoming a messenger and public figure.

Energetic sovereignty is the only means for every individual to move into his/her own Divine Sovereign Creatorship. No information, intel nor description of the different aspects of the false matrix is going to address and restore distortions in the inner planes, which is what is ultimately perpetuating the existence of a 3D artificial reality.

This brings all the power back to the Self. The Portal to the New Earth is Me and You. It is every brave, true and alive person who is choosing to take up the mantle of responsibility for the healing and co-creation of our reality.

~ ✻ ~

All the Beauty and Magic of the World cannot be accessed through merely the mind. Information can be regurgitated and shared through the mind, but true connection and collaboration with the Aliveness of the world can only be experienced through the Soul. Without cultivating our individual Pure Heart's Intent of Love and Reverence for the Sacred Creation, knowledge becomes be a seductive power which destroys worlds.

For this reason, at this time on Earth, the most important task that we all have to share is the Reclamation and Remembrance of our intimate connection to the Aliveness of the World and the Humility that comes through this connection. This is our Portal to Ascension.

Without a focus on this one and only important task, one can easily get lost in ego games of the many new age spirituality cults. Awakening is not a purely mechanical process, but one that is colourful, textured, manifold and multi-dimensional. It is a journey of experiencing the Love Affair between our Self and the greater Self, the One Aliveness which penetrates All the Cosmos.

The Meaning of Life is Creation itself. If we can understand that the Aliveness which penetrates All That Is is both the Creator and the Created, we can begin to experience the consciousness which moves our Soul as the same which moves through the All. Here we find ourselves experiencing 7D consciousness.

In this perspective, ascension is an inward process of cultivating spiritual and emotional maturity and elevating our level of consciousness. This inward process then allows us to experience Heavenly Realities external to us, as the reality is an infinite dance between the Creator and the Created, the within and without.

This understanding destroys all illusion of separation and duality, illusions which have been hijacked and used as loopholes to enslave and torture Life beyond what is necessary to grow through suffering and pain. Illusions which teach us that an external power is greater than our own, that anything can control, enslave or perpetuate lack and fear in our own world. Illusions which convince us that we are anything less than Divine Sovereign Creator Beings of Magnificence, Beauty and Splendor.

~ ❀ ~

CHAPTER 13

The Starseed Mission & the Stages of Starseed Awakening

Lucidity and depth of seeing and understanding multidimensionally is the beginning of creating solutions, technologies and healing systems which get to the root of the issues we face on Earth. That root is planetary creative / sexual enslavement. The big boss is gone - which means there's no war. But the healing and building of bridges is still up to us -

Earthstar Healers

In truth there is no separation between Star and Earth. Star is a frequency of light and consciousness which penetrates physicality as well as all realms. Many people think "starseeds" do not feel at "home" on Earth, when in actuality, it is the vibration of the false matrix which does not feel like "home".

The organic vibration of Nature streams undisturbed pure cosmic consciousness which flows through all organic Life in living physicality. This is the same Life energy which penetrates all things in all dimensions, and as this light originates from the stars, I like to call this frequency "star". In this case, a "starseed" is someone who recognizes and embodies this frequency wherever they come from, and would recognize this congruence amongst all expressions of Love in the Universe.

I'm painting a feeling here in which "star" and "earth" are inseparable. Star is describing the frequency of Consciousness which gives Life to Matter. The natural gravitation of a soul towards the Embodiment of this Consciousness is what makes us a "starseed". We have come as boost of Cosmic Consciousness for this planet at this time for Universal Consciousness Evolution.

Awakening to the Truth of our Cosmic Consciousness is only the beginning. Many in the new age community get stuck here and live as floating blasts of light intermixed with chaos and confusion, unable to anchor or create anything substantial. Not many humans in the recent histories of Earth have allowed this consciousness to percolate through the entire body to be "embodied", yet this is the only way to experience our True Divine Creatorship inside our human bodies.

In the following segments of this chapter I describe the various stages and processes of Embodiment "starseeds" must venture through to actualize our Self and our Mission. My own experiences of inner and outer awakening happened concurrently through experiences which were created and guided by my higher self. This allowed my creative intelligence to deduct many things with my embodied human brain intelligence, this is what "c0-creation" looks like.

We are not blind soldiers being sent into a dark battlefield with only our ear-piece and commander sitting in the sky to direct us. We are embodied galactic beings here to co-create this mission with our inter-dimensional selves and helpers. Through our healing, meditation and embodiment, we can perfectly access our own soul and higher self and the template and codes of our own mission and awakening. For this reason I do not "channel" "higher beings" to ask intimate questions about my own life and purpose.

Earthstar refers to the Earthstar Chakra beneath our feet which connects us into the Living planet. When I tune in psychically, I witness the Earthstar chakras of all living beings create a network of light filaments which communicate and share energy and information with each other. Similar to the mycelium network and the root systems of trees, humans are not separate from these organic networks of communication and life - just like in Avatar!

The epic cohesion, respect and love that is experienced in the unification of all life creates a powerful field of living light, rendering the Earth a Star.

The disconnection from Life, the Living Planet and Cosmic Consciousness humanity currently experience en masse is a great sickness which is perpetuated by viruses of consciousness and belief. The hidden controllers of humanity created systems on systems of lies which kept humanity from accessing the Truth of Nature.

Our collective connection to Reality and our Planetary existence can be symbolized by our Earthstar chakra. The distortion of our roots extend far and deep, from the food we are taught to eat, the social structures we're taught to behave within, to the degradation of Sexuality and Energy Exchange. Matters of the soul, sovereignty and true divinity are distorted by religious programming. Henceforth Humanity became severed from the True Reality, and our energies were siphoned into the creation of a false reality.

Satanic ritual abuse, military mind control, abduction programs, mind control through TV and radio frequencies, colonialism, genocide, racial injustice, poverty and fear propaganda, are all gradients of the same sickness. These things damage and degrade our individual and collective DNA which continue from generation to generation. This sickness degrades our ability to access and experience our Cosmic Creator Consciousness, which is what allowed humanity to become creatively enslaved.

The reality within which this Great Sickness reigns is what I refer to as the false or artificial matrix. The artificial matrix hijacks human sovereignty through influencing our consciousness and our energy body with fear and manipulation, to make choices which perpetuate the false reality.

This false reality which feeds its tyrant kings cannot exist without our tacit consent and participation. Coming into Energetic Sovereignty and Mastery is how we withdraw our creative energy in all dimensions, and become foundationally empowered to Create a New World based on Love, Freedom, Joy, Beauty and Divine Co-Creation.

This process of Energetic Sovereignty and Mastery then becomes our first and foremost mission, because our true Purpose can only emerge and become fulfilled through this process. Through our inner alchemy, we experience our own soul's preferences, interests, gifts and desires, thus discover the avenue of restoration and co-creation we'd like to anchor in.

Restoring all dimensions from the false reality to the organic reality is the foundation of our mission. This inspires me to study and assess how expressions of "health care systems" are distorted in the false reality, how these distortions affect humanity, and thus how through the refinement, synthesis and expression of my Creative Energy and Time I can create projects which are organic, higher expressions of "healthcare systems" in the 3D world.

My soul has a deep devotional interest in the Mechanics of Creation. In the higher dimensions I exist as a light-field geneticist. Higher dimensional understanding of Science is very different than commonly understood here on Earth. To Know and Understand the creation, so to contribute to its ever expanding Love and Beauty is the highest honor one can obtain in the living oneness of the Universe. I have experienced many lifetimes as a healer, shaman, and oracle, and these skills allow me to deduce that in this lifetime I would like to make contributions to these aspects of society.

This cohesiveness in understanding and creation can only come after a certain level of "knowledge of self". Through a knowing of my own soul, preferences, skills and etc, my embodied soul inside this vessel is empowered to create on my own free will and intelligence in authenticity, which is the secret sauce of Creation.

This level of integration only occurred after 7 years of deep devotion to healing, energetic sovereignty and mastery as my priority. Until this level of clarity is reached, we cannot be sure we are acting and creating from a place of harmony. Without deeply understanding and accessing our own multi-dimensional and energetic nature, how could we create a world in resonance with our Divine Creativity?

We come into embodiment of divine knowledge, then this level of consciousness will be weaved into anything we create. Without having a clear and sovereign vessel and energy system, we will not be able to fluently create consistently. Without consistent access to creativity, how could anchor the foundations necessary to evolve a whole planetary reality?

In order to create foundational change and creations of excellent magnitude, we need to have a clear and sovereign vessel. With this clear and sovereign multidimensional vessel, we can anchor and create Massive foundations and change to the 3D reality because our ability to create will match the truth of our Soul, a Divine Creator Being incarnate.

This is why mechanically, healing our self heals the world. A truly Embodied Emanating Divine Creator Being Incarnate operating inside the Whole Body, anchored in through the Root and Earthstar Chakras are directly co-creating with the forces of Nature motivated by Love. Our clear vessel allow this Force to move through us with Clarity and Power, allowing us access to creativity unimaginable.

Many starseeds and lightworker stay circulating inside the new age community, which is both a brilliant place of nurturance and a cage. While the new age community allow us the space and encouragement to be our "crazy" and "unconventional" selves, some get stuck in this safe place forever, and never get around to fulfilling our mission.

I believe at some point in our embodiment journey, the starseed is empowered and grounded enough to realize that we did not come here to jerk off our proverbial spiritual superiority, but to apply our Cosmic Consciousness to Real World Issues.

How can we apply our Divine Creatorship to manifest in the physical reality organizations which reaches out to hold the hands of All of Humanity? How can we Alchemize our Divine Creatorship into palpable, physical structures which dramatically improve the collective reality for All of Life? This is the true Mastery that we have come to experience in the evolution of our own Soul.

Learning of our Multidimensionality, and how this multidimensionality have been degraded and taken advantage of on a Collective and Planetary Level brings us into a level of lucidity, to know that all of humanity will reclaim and restore our divinity, energetic sovereignty and mastery. This lets us see that there is still much work to do. And we are here to do it.

The only way we can create real, palpable, foundational change to this physical world is to bring our Cosmic Consciousness fully into our Physical Body. This is made possible through clearing, healing, and restoring all distortions which are in the way. Our complete healing and integration is a beginning, from which point the Game of Life Truly commences as the Divine Creator Beings which we are.

Am I a Starseed?

Since beginning to offer Starseed Embodiment classes and sessions in 2017 I have worked with hundreds of fascinating lightworkers, hailing from Sirius, Pleiades, Alpha Centaurus, Andromeda, the elemental and angelic realms deeply connected to the Earth, and beyond. Basically what I've found is that if you are asking this question, then there is something in the exploration of "starseed"edness which is meant for you.

My working definition of a Starseed is a soul who incarnates with more than average amounts of cosmic and origin consciousness in tact, with a deeply felt inner purpose to assist in the healing and evolution of planet Earth and Humanity. We can say that everyone is a starseed, since we all originate from the same cosmic source. However my intention in using this word the way I do is to offer certain people who feel an especially alive sense of this word the space to come into empowerment through self recognition.

While in some sense, all people are "star beings", at this time on Earth some souls have chosen to have a more accelerated and intense cosmic experience than others. It is their soul's mission, capability and current stage of soul evolution to awaken ahead of the masses and participate in a more proactive fashion. For this reason I am using this word to this group of people as an activation code, a DNA phire letter, to empower us to come into our full power.

I also use the word "starseed" to describe people who are born into certain magical genetic lineages, who have natural abilities and spiritual knowledge from their previous lives of diligent spiritual practices and studies on Earth. The "star" part of "starseed" doesn't necessary have to appoint to a place in the cosmic sky, but rather a frequency of consciousness. A universal level of understanding of Creation. Galactic Consciousness. Original Angelic Consciousness.

This is not to exclude anyone from this process, as all people have a higher self that is cosmic in Nature and connected to the universal creation, and all people can use this word and this embodiment process to achieve higher and purified versions of self. However if you are someone who is awakening at this time, chances are you are a forerunner, contracted to awaken ahead of time, to undergo your healing process ahead of the masses in order to hold space and assist others to come.

Why you have awakened before the others is a sign of your spiritual maturity. Due to your past life experiences, you are equipped to process more trauma and distorted energy consciousnessly than others, thus are more capable of moving through extraordinarily dark and traumatic information whereas another might become stricken with fear.

This does not make you superior or better than others, it's simply a matter of maturity. Suppose your house caught on fire, you wouldn't expect your 5 year old to take charge of the situation and ensure everyone's safety - this would be the responsibility of the adults in the home. You wouldn't feel superior or better than the 5 year old either, it's the same sort of thing.

In my work I have discovered many different souls from different realms, dimensions, galaxies and star systems, with myriad different ways of going about this unified Purpose of Service to Life. Some examples are human incarnate of predominantly elemental beings who lived most previous lifetimes as elemental spirits like rivers and forests, refuge souls from galactic wars coming from different refuge planets here on a mission to heal and resolve galactic karma, and even other beings from other universes here to evolve through high level service to Creation.

What all these beings have in common is a natural attraction towards spiritual perspectives on reality, and esoteric healing modalities and knowledge. The 3D mind controlled reality is just too absurd for these souls to accept. Most of these beings were born with extrasensory abilities and a natural affinity for other realms and worlds particularly in dreams and fantasies. Many grew up in difficult family situations and develop psycho-emotional illness due to the vast vibrational difference between the environment and the authentic self.

While there are just as many paths and missions as there are starseeds on Earth now, there are certain unifying factors which all starseeds share - it is the process of remembering our true selves, where we come from and what we are doing here. Our collective mission at the end of the day, despite which sector or dimension we have agreed to participate, is to truly Wake Up to the multi-dimensional Divinity of our own being.

The juxtaposition of this innate Divinity and the way things were in the artificial world makes it easy for us to wake up. Upon waking up, we will have a lot of healing and excavation work to do to restore the mechanics of our own soul-body complex. This allows us to anchor our authentic soul into our body, effectively anchoring new codes and frequencies of expression. It is only through this process of healing and embodiment that we can create concrete change and healing in the human collective experience and planetary sphere.

The Different Waves of the Starseed Mission

Different generations, waves and teams of Starseeds incarnating at different times had very different jobs. In my exploration of this phenomena, it feels that there is a great deal of oneness and cooperation in the fabric of our collective mission.

A large portion of older generation starseeds' sole mission was to just be here. During these early years in the 40s and 50s, the collective consciousness and vibration on Earth was still far too low for them to do much. On top of this, the Earth was clouded inside a field of density and the exact situation was difficult for galactic and cosmic beings to perceive. Meaning we knew the frequency of what was happening on Earth, but none of the details.

We felt the frequency consciousness and energy had fallen in this quadrant of the Universe, but we did not know that mind control was being propagated onto the masses, that vaccines and GMOs were being produced to create mass genetic degradation, we didn't know consciously the specific vehicles which propagated the frequency fence.

So the first wave of incarnating as early as the 40s and as late as the 60s both had the most treacherous and confusing jobs. Most clients I've worked in this age group had ET communication but had no one to talk to about them for 40+ years. Most of these clients always felt they are a bit "out of this world" and didn't quite belong in mainstream culture, and also knew they were here for some sort of mission.

The bravery of these souls who chose to incarnate first are truly heroic, as just by them landing here and bringing the vibration of their soul here to the extent that they did, made massive shifts in the frequencies on Earth. Just by being here, outdated foundations were cracked and new levels of light penetrated into the Earth. In conjunction with the solar system entering the photon belt, these cosmological events opened a window for astronomical shift to occur.

On top of this, many galactic aspects of these first wavers also continuously sent ground information up to our collectives and lightships, which allowed the starseed mission to encode more and more detailed "anti-viral coding" into future generation starseeds. Not only do these new codes safe-guard younger starseeds from mind control and consciousness degradation, they also create certain levels of immunity to toxicity and genetic degradation.

This allows the new generations of starseeds a higher platform to initiate their missions with far less damage to their vessels and consciousness than previous generations had to deal with. For this heroic act I give those courageous first waver souls my respect and gratitude!

Now a second wave of starseeds are coming in mostly from the 60s to the 80s. The majority of clients I work with in this age range rolled their way through time into matrix jobs always feeling like there was something missing. At some point later in life, these beings get hit with a potent wave of activation and begin to become agitated at their jobs, and feel the calling of something bigger than themselves. Yet because their antibodies and coding was still not as advanced as the later generation starseeds, they have a harder time overriding the programming and "just jumping" off the false matrix band wagon.

Many in this age group become spiritual healers, teachers and organizers which created the foundation for the New Age / Awakening Community. They ensured the popularization of spirituality that became more socially acceptable. This was an extremely necessary foundation to create and establish because it become the perfect nursery and training ground for the future generation of starseeds.

Many in this age group were tasked with generating financial wealth and foundations to support the budding creativity of future generation starseeds. However many got whirled too deeply into the false matrix and the programming suppressed their capacity to understand their role and thus fulfill their mission.

The false matrix ideologies of lack and competition made it difficult for many to truly open their hearts and generosity to participate in something greater than themselves. These failed missions serve as examples and information for coding antiviral in the future generations of starseeds

In my own life, I am fortunate enough to have received the intergenerational support of my star family, through Stu, Harlan, Jeff and a small handful of other mature adults. This coding is strong in my own system as it's very natural for me to hold space for a younger starseed, to offer them my financial and emotional stability for them to shine.

If you're an older generation starseed, support your younger generation starseeds financially and foundationally. If you have developed a film, event, music or whatever company in your years and expertise, open your mind to allow the younger generation starseeds to blossom and showcase their powers, perspectives and wisdom. Use the foundation you have created to encourage the growth and development of the new starseeds because we are not here to struggle to get to where you are. In our collective oneness, the young are here to shine on the platforms the old have already created. This is how generational evolution is supposed to grow organically. This is all a part of the plan.

I say this not to get handouts as a young person, but because this is how I think. I intend to create massive abundance through the mastery of the mechanics of creation and my own creatorhood. In these years of my journey I have always shared my abundance with promising brilliant starseeds, as my investment of time and money becomes beauty and magic in the World through their embodiment and empowerment. This is of more value than dollars can ever be.

Through the amassing of abundance and grounded creativity, I intend to offer foundation and nurturance to the future generations of starlings still to incarnate.

I think about how much acceleration I have received from having a nurturing and peaceful environment which supports my embodiment and planetary work. The fact that a first wave starseed purchased this land in New Mexico, left all his retirement money to it and intended for it to nurture me, a future generation starseed, is creating a universe of difference in my life and the level of work I'm able to produce and share with the world.

In my own journey, I have become disheartened many times experiencing the opposite energy from "elders". Elders who believe adamantly that they must "teach" me, indoctrinate me, put me into a box. Adults who are jealous of my nature, and believe I have to "suffer the way they did" to "deserve what they have now." Instead of feeling joyful that I am here in coherence and embodiment, they felt threatened or fearful of losing their own spotlight and abundance.

There are many distortions we are beginning to heal as a global family and community, and it goes so far deeper than just the surface levels that we are barely scratching now. All Is Self is not a mental or intellectual concept, but something that remains true in all facets and levels of life we explore this word in.

As we roll into the late 80s and 90s, the solar system enters the photon-belt entirely, which allowed for even higher vibrational starseeds to incarnate. As the foundation for mass awakening had been set by previous generations, this also created a fertile playground for the new generation to fulfill their missions. The phenomena of indigo and crystal children became popularized, and some of these children were born to first and second wave starseeds themselves.

Many starseeds I know and have worked with in this age group woke up to their missions and galactic heritage at extremely young ages as early as middle school. Since they have access to infinite information on the internet, many begin to dive into spirituality, plant medicine, and conspiracies at a young age - most come into complete awakening in their 20s. With their coding it's actually quite difficult to stay asleep.

These beings go through a period of detox from the false matrix in order to fully come into our own soul embodiment, and at this point re-merges back into the "mundane" world to bring corrections and societal transition support technologies back to the masses. This can appear as establishing oneself professionally in grounded 3D environments while still staying true to our self. This only becomes possible when we are fully anchored in our true self. The external can no longer influence us subconsciously, and we gain the empowerment to influence the external.

There are also special missions that souls took to incarnate and participate in certain experiences which required their partial unconsciousness. Many beings whose souls chose intentional life paths into politics, technology, military and education inside the false matrix in order to perceive and send up information to our galactic missions. Many took on positions of power in the 3D to empower and uplift this foundation for the future generation starseeds. Many of these beings became whistleblowers, truth tellers and pillars of stability for the mass timeline migration.

At this point in time, there is a merging or shedding of time. The Starseed Mission is shifting from a silent, undercover and planning phase to a full-on, outwardly in action phase in which we are beginning to interact with mass consciousness and society consciously and intentionally. There will soon come a time when our presence on Earth will be known by all, and we will be welcomed for our gifts, wisdom and motivation to Heal, Assist and Uplift humanity.

The manifestation of this reality and the speed at which it manifests will rely mostly on the level of integration and embodiment the ground crew exhibits and sustains. This means all hands on deck. No matter which generation of the starseed mission a soul had originally incarnated into, if a soul still chooses to continue to participate, the task on hand becomes the same. Coming into full integration and embodiment of our Soul and shifting to operate in higher dimensional mechanics of reality.

Like the understanding I received when working at the addictions recovery place, that I am here to be of service to the people and the people do not owe me their acceptance and understanding, integration is the difference between being taken for a raving lunatic, and a wise philosopher.

In the earlier stages of our awakening, we can be defensive and even argumentative of our own beliefs and dispositions. Through emotional maturity, spiritual growth and embodiment, we no longer subconsciously seek external validation. This allows us to communicate in a more grounded and comprehensible manner, which ultimately opens the door to our diplomatic and helpful presence on Earth.

Higher Self Embodiment as a Walk-In Process

Since the beginning of my awakening I have felt the sensation of my true soul 'walking-in'to my body. Not a foreign or a different soul than one originally assigned to this body. Perhaps simply that my higher-self and true soul memories were cascading into the 3D. In my healing work now I find that this is a structural process that all starseeds go through - or can use as a perspective to gage our embodiment process.

When we are born, we learn and develop our chakras in segments of 7 years beginning with the root chakra. Meaning in the first 7 years of our life, we predominantly discover, explore and define our root chakra. Then in the 8-14 year, we move onto the sacral and so on. If we grew up in the false matrix, then our energy center and knowledge associated with those chakras will be programs of mind control and degradation which align with the false reality.

For example, the majority of humans are exposed to survival fear and lack mentality through our environment and parents in our youth. By the time children are 5, they are already asked the question: "what do you want to be when you grow up?" - this question implies that at some point one will have to get a job which makes one money in order to survive in our societal system. Not to mention the monetary stress the majority of parents are in, a strong vibration of fear and lack. All of this inscribes an artificial pressure in our root chakra.

Another example is the false education of sexuality we receive in the public school system as well as mass media, to portray sex as both something degrading, shameful, secretive and fearful. Compounded by shameful and repressive societal and religious programs surrounding sexuality our parents may have, this inscribes deep detrimental blockages into the sacral chakra which obscure the flow of creative energy and relating, creating pain and trauma.

These examples of distortions within these chakras will not resonate with our higher dimensional aspects of self. When our soul begins to embody and operate the physical vessel, our authentic energy will not be able to take up the space in which the distortions exist. So in order for our higher dimensional aspects to fully embody inside our body those artificial energies, programs and belief systems will have to be processed, deleted and restructured.

Our society also deems any sort of intuitive and mystical communication between realms as "fantasy and not real". When a young child communicates with fairies, elementals and the Earth's spirit, often times they are told this is "just imagination" or not real. This becomes a foundational belief inscribed into our "root - understanding of reality". As an adult, this directly shuts down our intuition and ability to connect interdimensionally.

As you can imagine then, there are so, so many layers to this deprogramming. Imagine the number of generations of ancestors that we know who have lived inside poverty, strife, war and societal mind control. Those programs or vibrational patterns are in fact passed down through parental DNA and will also require our attention to resolve.

I believe this deprogramming and healing process is the most vital and powerful work we can do for our self and our humanity at this time, because without this process we are not sovereign and we perpetuate the continuation of these energies in our reality. This is the intention and purpose of my next project "Advanced Lightwork: Medicine for the Great Sickness" in which we will explore the myriad dimensions of these false programs, and actively work on self-healing and restoring our original energy system.

Every thought, movement and action that we take is continuing the co-creation of our shared reality. When we think, move and act with running programs of mind control regardless of how subtle, we perpetuate the false matrix. This is both dense and liberating, because it gives the power back to us to change the world from the inside out.

In 2013 my team informed me that the migration of timelines and the restructuring my reality from the artificial 3D timelines, to my soul's organic timelines was going to take around 7 years. This would only be true if I devoted my entire life to this process, and made it my top priority above all else. This meant that 7 years from my first moment of remembering in March of 2013, I would be walking around in my body, actually integrated and in expression as my true Self.

To some this would sound like a long time, but in relation to the length of our lifetime, and the centuries these artificial conditions and viruses have lived through our genetic lineage, this is a reasonable amount of time to undergo a complete reprogramming process. This reprogramming process must take place in the many layers and dimensions of our consciousness, somatic body and DNA.

To others you might think, I have been awake for nearly two decades and I'm still not integrated! This can also be the case if reprogramming and embodiment is not yet your one and only goal, and priority in life. Some people think well Xi you are so lucky that you get to "travel and be yourself". To that I say they have not seen the other side of spending full days every week in sheer agony purging intergenerational and collective trauma of rape and injustice.

In those first years I often found myself in an energetic lull, my psychic senses flying in streams of light while my physical body daydreamed. In these luls I would type "migration of timelines and the restructuring of reality..." as if a message to myself that this was happening in the undercurrents.

From my experience and also what I have seen in hundreds of client sessions, is that the process of Starseed Awakening is very similar to a walk-in experience. I feel that thinking of it in this way is helpful to the integration process because it helps us remember that our whole self and everything we brought here in the form of gifts, abilities, wisdom and knowledge are stored inside our soul. In order for this soul to flower and unleash itself fully, it needs to have all the room inside our consciousness and our body.

The starseed embodiment process usually begins in the higher chakras, and is a process of moving downwards through the body. I believe the reasons for this are that firstly, the soul star is above the body, secondly we awaken through our mind's awareness, and thirdly the energies in the lower chakras are much denser, difficult to penetrate and take longer to process.

In the first year of my awakening I remember having constant tension on the top of my crown, with brief elated moments of complete openness as if my cranium was the wide open sky. Then the years following I felt my "soul" which is a distinct yet familiar vibration of being different from the muggle self, inside my head but just above the neck. I felt like my body was submerged under water and I didn't feel this lightness could penetrate lower into my body.

As I went through years of deprogramming the hidden distortions and traumas in my body, I would notice this "soul" vibration filling up more and more of my body every time I check in. I have distinct memories of coming down to my liver, and especially the sacral regions which massive amounts of purging and healing was necessary to get any deeper into my own body. I also remember new aspects of self coming into my body for the first time and feeling distinctly those aspects genuinely bewildered by what they saw, as they'd never been to Earth before.

This process of embodiment took place quite literally inside my body as I moved through these 7 years of epic adventure which are journalled here in this book.

To my understanding, migration from the false reality to the organic reality was very simple. It meant completely reshaping the landscape and background of our life from the way of life we were born into, to a life with freedom to create and experience that which we choose. Most people were born into deep conditioning that we have to sacrifice our time and energy in order to survive. This conditioning reaches far and wide into all the different crevices of our lives.

The organic reality to me looks like having absolute freedom to choose how we spend our time in each moment while staying devoted through our hearts to loving co-creation with All that is. It means being free from all levels of mind control and enslavement, purified from all layers of artificial personalities created by the artificial world, and being absolutely free to express our self as our Soul.

For the Starseed, this process invariably leads to our fulfillment of our purpose and missions on Earth. Without going through this process, there simply isn't enough room in our consciousness and body to hold the magnitude of Aliveness which we truly are. For this reason, the process of purification, healing and embodiment is the most effective journey to initiating our Starseed Mission on Earth.

As we are multidimensional beings, the process of remembering my Self coincided with the process of my self discovering my environment - Earth. In order to discover our Purpose, we have to know who we are, where we are, and how the who and the where interact.

Through the culmination of my experiences in these 7 years, I have derived a coherent and complete understanding of the Starseed Mission. As a geneticist who played part pre-incarnation in creating codes for starseeds to journey here, I feel that I am in a good position to share my perspective of the Starseed Mission.

I remember all those years ago when I discovered the Starseed materials online, it all seemed very theatrical. Many were talking about different origins of starseeds and their personality traits. A lot of light and fluffy exclamations that we were here to change the world. But through all the youtube videos I watched and channelings and books I read about star people, not once did I read about the starseed mission in a grounded manner.

I never found embodied starseeds talking about the actualization of our mission on Earth, only information about starseeds and the ascension itself, with words, but not the action of the mission itself. Over the years I realized the very sad fact that there is a lot of infiltration, false transmissions and distraction campaigns in the new age and truther community to capture and stall the starseed from truly initiating our missions.

The simple truth is that we can only fully access and fulfill our mission once our Soul is fully embodied. Penetrating through the lower chakras require moving through the necessary karmic, societal and ancestral traumas and distortions which can take many years of focussed intense work. Once we have reprogrammed our lower chakras and are flowing our authentic energy through them, we become manifesting masters of divine creative genius, motivated by love and compassion.

In this place of creative genius, energetic mastery and correct motivation, the pathway to the New Earth will be a joyful dance in the playground of Life.

The Stages of Starseed Awakening

I will now break down my assessment of the Stages of Starseed Awakening. Please note that as we are multidimensional beings, this process will be individual and unique to everyone. Many of these steps may be happening concurrently and you might experience some steps before or after others. This is a general flow of our awakening and embodiment process.

The human mind and our different inner fragmented parts do a great job at making excuses for why we should remain in certain stages instead of moving forward and focusing on our own healing and complete restructuring of our reality. Bear that in mind as you proceed!

1. Asleep Inside the Matrix

This first stage is pretty self explanatory. Most of us have gone through it. We were born with our gifts and abilities intact. Then we went to kindergarten, we ate junk food, we watched TV, got funneled into high school and maybe even went to college and got a job which had nothing to do with our soul or our personal fulfillment.

We had a personality which lived inside these artificial institutions, partly based on our insecurities and traumas, and had friends who interacted with this personality with whom we shared superficial interactions.

For the majority of us this was actually an important period of our life. The forgetting of our true self and our magic allowed us to physically experience the pain and degradation all of humanity experienced. Many of us experienced mental illness or addictions, and this ultimately served as a crash course on genetic degradation.

Through our first hand experience with different levels of mind control, we gain the experience of healing our self and liberating our self. This not only gives us the gift of empathy with the masses, but the ability to assist others through this process as well.

The majority of starseeds, especially those born after the 80s and 90s, incarnated with antiviral which protected us against certain levels of mind control. These protective codes would have felt like to us that something was "off" about reality. We might grow up inside the institutions but we always felt a level of distrust towards the powers that were. At some point these codes fully activate triggering us into the next stage.

2. Confronting Discomfort - Assessing and questioning the reality

At some point, being asleep in the matrix began to feel very off. Some may even develop especially adverse reactions to the false matrix in the form of mental or psycho-physical illness. The "off"ness could no longer be ignored and the discomfort of having to deal with the false matrix, a very foreign and distorted frequency, peaks into a confrontation.

This is the first spark of our soul beginning to awaken inside our body. This happens in our awareness and our intellect, the first part of our self that notices the oddness of our reality. The discomfort we perceive to be caused by our external environment is also the discomfort our true soul feels inside our body infested with artificial programs, parasites and implants.

This discomfort could be experienced as an exhaustion from our false matrix job or university degree, or severe emotional disconnection from our biological family members, or a combination of such triggers. In order to find relief or healing from this discomfort, we begin to look for answers that question the very foundation of our reality.

This usually leads into one of two directions, with lots of intermixing of the two. For those who experienced any sort of illness as their trigger, they might start to look into natural and holistic healing modalities. Through this they might discover energy healing and feel a resonance with exploring other dimensions of reality beyond 3D. This might lead one into the new age community where they find some answers about their spiritual and cosmic uniqueness.

The second direction takes us into the quest for knowledge and truth. We begin to see that the institutions like the medical, pharmaceutical and educational are really self serving and not operating in integrity. This leads us into researching the powers of control existent on Earth and this might lead one into the truther & disclosure community.

3. Synchronicity & Initial Activation Blast

In all the hundreds of clients I have worked with, when we spoke about the initial moments of awakening, there was always a unique and special period of time which major synchronicities and heightened spiritual awareness surrounded them. Almost like an intense blast of spiritual energy which makes it very difficult for anyone to ignore and continue to repress true intuitions and feelings.

This orb of awakening begins to grow in our awareness and we begin to take notice of synchronicity and other energetic occurrences in our reality. We start to notice the disconnectedness of people around us more intensely, and also perhaps repeating numbers.

This can be experienced as a kundalini blast, an extraordinary circumstance in life which creates a sharp turn of events, a near death experience, a death or birth in the family, even one or several psychedelic journeys. It could be a period of heightened dream activity or self-healing, or a combination of a bunch of these.

This blast of activation energy is like a fever which burns away a layer of debris in our energy body to allow this orb of growing awareness to take hold in our mind. However it moves through our lives, it anchors us into a new quest to discover our true purpose, and the true nature of reality around us.

4. Deep Dive into Truth & The New Age

As this orb of awakening anchors into our body during this intense period of activation, one might find oneself almost obsessed with everything related to the awakening. This can look like purchasing a lot of physical detox products and books, watching endless disclosure or channeling videos on youtube, and diving into everything which was hidden before.

This process can take a few months to years, as it is actually an entrainment of our subconscious mind. In order for us to operate in the higher frequencies of "new earth" we have to restructure the frequency of our neural-networks and foundational brain waves which had been programmed for so many years inside the false matrix frequencies.

The tricky aspect of this stage of awakening is that we are still lingering in our cerebral regions of our body. The light is piercing through our awareness in our studies and intellectual understanding, but not yet able to move through the rest of our body as we are still too dense.

Usually at this stage we are mostly looking at things outside of our self - like disclosure of the secret elite and military operations, receiving channeled information from disincarnate angels and beings, and beginning to acquire healthier non GMO food. Because we haven't gone through our inner work yet, this is a place of awakening many can get trapped in because wounded aspects of self (the infamously named "ego") trick us into believing we have awakened and "arrived".

Making a relation to my story, this phase of awakening would be the period of time I spent at my parents house listening to quantum healing podcasts and enjoying galactic dream adventures. I was beginning to access vocabulary like "5D" and beginning to sense what that could mean, but I didn't have any activated "5D" skills nor knew how my own mission will fit in with the rest of the world.

I was having lots of conversations with my friends and siblings about the evil corporations of the world (facebook is great for this) and feeling glib about all that I "knew" that they didn't. I had no real solutions for any of these issues because the only solutions to dismantling the artificial reality come from becoming absolutely Authentically Soul Embodied, and I didn't yet know that nor how to get there.

So based on all of these facets, it is easy to see how one can get stuck at this stage without much desire to move forward until another confrontation happens. One thing I have observed in the awakening community is this next phase, which is really kind of like a side step.

5. Righteous Anger or Defeat & Premature, Misguided or Incomplete Action

Upon discovering the atrocities that happen on Earth, propagated by the elite and military groups, yet still running certain 3D programs of action, many become motivated by their fear and anger. One may join protests, and attend expensive UFO conferences which may be infiltrated by the military itself. Some experience a deep depression in discovering certain truths and again repress intuitive feelings and go back to the comforts of forgetfulness.

As we understand, everything is frequency in interaction. An awakened mind does not equate to the demolition of false matrix belief systems and programs running in our subconscious and our body. So without an empowered soul presence, our programs lead us into creating situations, events and projects which perpetuate the false matrix.

It is impossible to act in complete integrity to self if we are still ultra wounded, fragmented or disembodied and have not yet done much inner work. It's impossible to "create a new world" if we ourselves are running and expressing false matrix energies and programs, as this itself continues the creation of the old.

Here are still ignorant to the way reality truly functions and how our consciousness interacts with the fabric of reality. After all, this is the basis of our Creatorhood and the path of mastery, and is something that has been targeted for thousands of years, beaten and starved out of humanity. The reclamation and embodiment of this truth is what will actually change the world, not any amount of yelling and regurgitating fearful facts about the past.

Some lucky ones skip this stage altogether, and others experience it only mildly through being pulled into certain communities. Still others are actually agents of disinfo, and consciously or unconsciously motivated by social status, wealth and fame, perpetuating cultural distortion agendas.

Ultimately the starseed's true soul, multi-dimensional team and genetic phire-letters activate and we will no longer resonate frequencially with certain factions of the new age or truther community. This deep inner gnosis of All is Self, and the codes of Sovereign Creatorhood phires and shifts us into this next stage of awakening.

6. *Discovery of Mastery, Embodiment & Self-Healing*

Of all the clients, acquaintances and beings I have met in the awakening community, only a few nearly bypasses the previous stages of awakening entirely. I witnessed these people jump right into the Discovery of Mastery, Embodiment and self-healing after their initial confrontation and activation. They never forgot these innate truths of Reality, and as soon as they came online, they went right for the good stuff.

Some of these beings remain my greatest allies and teachers to date, as the first beings to remind me to awaken to my gnosis of "all is self".

This stage almost comes as its own activation, it's a sobering moment that might once again be a product of exhaustion. Exhaustion from the superficiality one continues to experience even inside the new age or truther communities - an exhaustion which pushes on to go further to say: "this is not all there is."

When the outwardly seeking of teachers, whistleblowers, intel and channelings become exhausting, we get moved into a sobering stillness. We remember the age old saying that "all we need is within" and begin to excavate our Self.

Usually this is when one discovers wayshowers and multi-dimensional energy healers, or truly begin to understand the messages these beings share. We are beginning to understand the energetic and cohesive nature of Reality.

We begin to recognize that our Sovereign Creator vessels are intricately connected to the fabric of reality. This knowledge or awareness of our Self and our own energetic make-up is the key to 'saving the world' after all. Only through the reclamation of our vessel and energy system can we be truly free of the false matrix, thus establishing the foundation for a new earth void of the artificial reality altogether.

The discovery of these truths again is only the beginning of this new stage of life, as the most difficult initiation of all is the stepping into of embodiment. We might intellectually understand that "all is self", we are "creator beings", and that the external is a projection of the internal. We might consciously know that GMOs are not healthy for our energy system. Yet integrating these knowings to update our moment to moment way of expressing and living our life is an entirely different discussion.

At this point of the game, it's all about our choices and our ability to exercise our free will for the evolution and benefit of our self and the whole. If we want to point fingers at child traffickers, can we honestly say that we have rescued and given love to all of our abandoned and fragmented inner children? If we want to point fingers at the GMOs, can we honestly say that we are nourishing our self with love and self honesty?

We recognize that this way towards empowerment and self responsibility is the only way to reclaiming our creatorship, and it is only through this reclamation that we can truly create a new world in the most effective and efficient manner.

This stage of our awakening might take even a few years to truly sink in before we are actively engaged in the next stage. The loops of "just one more cigarette" or "I'll start eating healthy tomorrow" or even "I'll just follow one more spiritual teacher" lingers. Concurrently we are actually getting all of our fragmented aspects of self on the same page, moving us towards stepping into deep commitment to our Self and thus the whole.

7. Deep Commitment to Restructuring Reality Inside-Out

Once the realization sinks in that no action in the external world will result in substantial change unless we go inside to reclaim our sovereign energy systems as creator beings, we soberly accept this as a priority in our life.

We stop becoming fearful at all news and intel regarding wars, politics, secret space programs, massive cosmic radiation, because we know the external is just a reflection of our inner reality. And we know that as long as we are actively restoring our design as humanity, we are doing the best that we can. The external reality could not betray us because we do not betray our self energetically.

This sobering moment might come after years of struggling and again becoming exhausted by seemingly endless fruitless battles. Despite all the "work" one is doing, one's life is still wrought with lack, depression, anxiety and miscommunication with others. This triggers us into the final option, going within.

We begin to adopt self healing practices, and being presently aware of our own energy, consciousness, thoughts and feelings become the new normal. When something happens in the external reality, we remember to check in with our self first.

In this dedicated practice we are actually making room. Finally dissolving the patterns, geometries and ways of expressing which were inauthentic to our soul, developed through our decades of being within the false matrix. This process opens up clogged up channels in the energy system, which allows our authentic soul self to flow through into our body.

We begin to realize the deep truth of "everything we need is within us" and how without excavating we can't ever access this original part of our self connected to the oneness, our past life and higher dimensional skills and knowledge. We begin to surrender and let go into the oneness. Discovering a dmension of the Law of One teachings experienced only through the process of self healing and cultivation.

8. Remembrance, Activation & Embodiment of "Soul-Self", Skills & Knowledge

By this phase of our awakening, we are feeling like an entirely different person than we were months or years ago. But this "new" person actually feels like a familiar being that has always been, and that the artificial personalities were a distant faded dream. In this new place of embodiment, we feel a deep seated inner peace which stems from our own knowledge of our self and the reality.

From this place of integration and peace, we might all of a sudden become aware of different multidimensional skills we have, or hobbies become of interest to us that never were before. We are feeling empowered in our new sense of self-knowledge, and we are no longer seeking validation and confirmation from the external reality to tell us about our self and our own mission here on Earth.

In this space, I feel galactic and activated, full of peace, love and light, yet not separate or out of touch from the devastations and distortions of the false matrix world. As we are of Oneness with All That Is, all dimensions and all of time-space - the currently unraveling false matrix reality is still a present reality in the Creation.

This false matrix is the source of alchemy, motivation and inspiration to Create pathways of Healing and Shift for All Beings on this Planet.

For example, my higher dimensional skills are of psionic seeing and healing, when I am guided to grid-work in big cities, I assess the current genetic degradation levels of the population as well as the collective consciousness of the grid in that location. As I run creative energy through my vessel, I will become inspired in love and joy, to create inventions, modalities and social support infrastructure to make a difference in those real people's lives.

I can only share this example as someone who is operating as a part of the "health care" team, but you can apply this concept to other areas of interest specific to you. What aspects of this reality are the most interesting to you? Education? Media? Enviroment? Permaculture? The prison system? Poverty?

As we are multidimensional beings, the understanding and solutions that we have for 3D issues are what's needed. As Einstein so famously said, no problem can be solved from the same level of consciousness that created it. Tthe embodiment of our expanded, higher levels of consciousness is the key to flipping this planet in a few generations like we signed up collectively to do.

This level of integration moves us into our completing stage of starseed mission activation: grounded and embodied 3D actions.

9. Grounded 3D Action Based on 5D+ Integrated Creative Intelligence

Integration looks like no longer any need to seek external validation for the truth of our own soul. As how we never have to google "do I have fingers", we no longer have to google "am I a starseed?" either.

Our galactic cosmic self is now operating our vessel, and anchored through the root and earthstar chakras, we begin to notice how energy is completely flowing through us, giving us a new Pow! in our creative abilities.

There's no one way to describe the infinite myriad of solutions, projects and bridges our starseeded collective will create in the healing of this world, as the process of creativity itself becomes an act of play and joy infused with the infinite creative potential of the divine soul. Embodied in our multi-dimensionality, there's no longer any one occupation or way of doing things we have to follow.

Can you open to the possibility of acquiring millions if not billions of dollars through your own inner mastery of the mechanics of creation? In correct alignment with true motivation for the liberation and fulfillment of All beings, this level of creative energy in the Earth plane can truly change the world.

In the early stages of integration, a lightworker or starseed may absolutely reject money, aligning with the belief that it is the root of all evil. As we are creator beings, we lend our consciousness to the creation of such a reality, and push away material stability and comfort for ourselves.

In truth this is a wounded reaction in the root chakra towards the reality as it is. It is a rejection of the reality thus a rejection of a part of our self that is seeking reconciliation. Can we begin to perceive money as one of the greatest spiritual teachers Humanity has ever received? Can we alchemize the reality of Money into something more loving through our use and perception of it, and can it become something that can accelerate our mission?

In my early 20s I despised money. I thought that all the world's evils were caused by having or not having of it. I spent 3 years of my life living without it, and on the loving grace of others. This was a great experience to have, however unsustainable. Looking back at this period of time, I still used money to purchase food, bus tickets, books and courses.

I used money to buy plane tickets and gas for my car to get me to where I needed to go to experience the activations that I did. In those cases money allowed me make those things happen. I thought it would be quite hypocritical to say, all money is evil, when it benefited me in a profound way.

I realized I held much resentment towards money, for all the love I thought it took from me by creating suffering in my friends and loved ones. For suffocating and not nourishing the homeless and communities of people all over the world who are in poverty. For seemingly favoring heartless psychopaths who enslave this world.

When I healed this resentment I realized that money wasn't favoriting the psychopaths, because money itself is just an object. The psychopaths took ownership of the Knowledge of Creation and made it occult. They blanked humanity's mind of our own knowledge of our divine creative power so they could keep this knowledge for themselves.

Naturally to recognize the Truth of our Divine Creatorship gives the power back to us. I can make money my friend through wielding my Divine Power as a Sovereign Creator Being in the physical. I realized that I can program an equation into my reality which would allow my level of physical material abundance to reflect that of my Divine Soul's Infinite Creativity.

I started to have dreams of creating million, billions and even trillions of dollars. I dreamt that with that money, we created thousands of creative living education and healing centres in every major city around the globe, to help all humans in their recovery from planetary rape and enslavement and reclaim our multidimensionality.

It's not to say that money won't eventually disappear, transmute into a completely different form of energy exchange, or totally dissolve into organic exchanges of energy. However in our current moment in time, the galactic councils of elders deem a redistribution of currency an important stepping stone in the healing of our world. It's one organizing function that could accelerate the union of forces.

As we anchor and ground in through our root and earthstar chakras, our perception of time slows down. The previous feelings of urgency and haste to "save the world" or "wake up the masses" refines into a peaceful, consistent, steady yet potent creative energy which is what is necessary to anchor massive projects and foundations. This is a symptom of balancing, opening and anchoring into the root chakra.

When I first received these visions of these healing centres, my human mind would begin to research locations, prices, draw up designs and wonder why it's not happening. Then I realized that the visions are a gift. That I myself am not actually responsible for doing anything but to be a witness to the magic of the One Universe moving through me.

I realized that my only job was to heal myself because this allows the universe to move through me more smoothly, and all people focussing on this one simple task is the only way we can accelerate planetary healing. I stopped trying to make things happen altogether and surrendered to the Perfect Orchestration of our Divine Oneness. Things started to happen faster and in a more profoundly mystical way than I could have ever conceived on my own.

We realize that our different energy centres process and experience time differently. And that without truly anchoring into our physical body (and that means clearing and healing our lower chakras of all trauma, distortions and misbeliefs), we are floating in the reality of intellectual information and knowledge. In this state we are without any means to alter the physical reality in great capacity. Anchored in the root we peacefully look upon the natural world, to recognize that all things have their seasons, and there's no way to rush the growth of the garden.

Channels to Embodied Masters

This is not a channeled passage from a disincarnate source. These are authentic perceptions of reality processed and integrated by a galactic star being living in physicality. I am a multi-dimensional galactic being incarnated in human form, as all of you reading this are. We are those beings channelled for wisdom and guidance, except we are actually here on the Earth.

How would those beings we channeled process and perceive our reality if they were down here in human bodies?

My take on the phenomenon of channeling is that it was a step of our starseed mission that was highly important in the first stages of our presence, and that the way we approach and perceive channeling will shift as our perception of our Self shifts.

The high vibrational energies of our higher aspects couldn't be anchored on Earth permanently during the first wave of incarnation, so channeling was one way those energies could still penetrate the density and be brought down here to begin their infusion into the Earth's grid.

The act of channeling implies that there is a force that is "outside" of "self" that is of higher knowledge and power than the being participating in the channeling act, and for a while this was true, because the embodied vibration could only be so different from the mass energy on Earth. However these true cosmic beings that were being channeled were actually higher dimensional aspects of our Self.

Now over decades of lightwork and as we entered the photon-belt in the 90s, the frequencies are much higher on Earth. This means what couldn't be embodied vibrationally decades ago, now can be. Higher aspect that we once had to channel, are becoming embodied to participate in the game of physicality full time now.

That wisdom and knowledge we once had to channel to access, are now accessible in the moment, through our thoughts, feelings, intuitions and actions, because we now have full access to those dimensional aspects of our self consciously living inside our body.

This is a fascinating transition as this brings our sovereignty and empowerment back inside our Self. The process of embodiment connects us to our own soul, higher self and higher dimensional aspects, where we begin to access our own library of wisdom and knowledge that we are bringing to the Earth - of levels that go far beyond any books that have been written in recent history.

Coming into Wholeness

One of the medicines which is flowing through this subchapter is that of false light dissolution. There are many lies and purposefully misleading concepts perpetuated in the new age spiritual community which are meant to capture and "glass ceiling" lightworkers and starseeds. My intention in sharing this medicine is in helping us reach the next level of our purpose and mission here on Earth by blasting through the false light and into our authentic expression of self.

A being of light doesn't necessarily have to dress in any way, nor speak in a light and airy manner, nor only use language inside a subculture. Light is the presence of conscious awareness. Conscious awareness is a light in the centre which moves and penetrates outwards in all directions. In the infinite directions this light moves, each line of light is a different dimension or perspective or aspect of reality which is perceived.

The state of being in which we have integrated the myriad directions of perception, enough to form sovereign, intelligent, grounded and soulful decisions which benefit the self and reality, can be stated as "enlightened" - it could also simply be called "adulthood" in a healthy world. In a healthy world, perceiving the reality and how we navigate through it is what is shared with each being upon arriving into the world. We would call that "school".

In this train of thought, "enlightenment" or "maturity" would only be the beginning of a creator's life, as we become briefed on the structures, mechanics and rules of the shared reality. It's a state of the soul being fully present inside the body, in full awareness of all the aspects of the inner and outer reality, a state of wholeness. Only at this point is any being fully informed in order to make authentic, intelligent and organic decisions and actions which come from the soul embodied in the present.

When we first awaken, we may only light up a few strands of the totality of this source of light. We might find starseed or lightworker materials, and begin to read spiritual texts. We might discover something about the secret space program, or the satanic ritual abuse cults of the elites, and dive deep into the disclosure sector. We might begin certain self-healing practices and realize that we are an interconnected collective holographic reality - and become bedazzled by the new age sector.

However, all of these individual strands are only that - pieces of the puzzle - it is only through slow cultivation of presence, embodiment and maturity that we begin to perceive all these pieces in a coherent and whole picture. Once we reach this coherence, our "purpose" and our "mission" become clear as day.

We move through this process of lighting up each strand individually, as our human mind is only capable of processing so much and our emotional body is only as mature as the experiences we have integrated and grown from. It would "blow a circuit" should we awaken to all the aspects of the multi-dimensional reality outside of the 3D all at once.

The process of integrating these myriad aspects of reality in order to achieve maturity requires time, intent and focus, and only achievable in good time if we make piercing through the illusions of our 3D reality our priority. Once we anchor in our honest and earnest intent, the universe, our own soul and higher self creates the pathway and situations for us to experience deeper and deeper levels of integration and wholeness.

The cultivation of "self" awareness, which includes both the inner and outer realities, becomes the one and only task until the self becomes fully present and whole - signaled by stable, confident, joyous and peaceful presence - not easily altered by any surprise nor seduced by drama.

In this state of wholeness, maturity and integration we gain the ability to respond to certain dire realities of our world with right action. The deeper this integration takes place, the greater impact this action can create in the healing of our world. Thus is shown the esoteric knowing of as within so without - as we heal ourself, we literally amplify our ability to heal the world.

All this is spiraling into the central truth that what keeps us from being lucid in our living waking dream is often our subconscious fears. Our childhood and adolescent traumas which may be deep and multi-faceted due to the disconnected world most of us grew up in keeping our awareness from grounding deep into our body.

The new age spiritual deceivers use this as the perfect leverage to convince people to stay above the heart - after all - who wouldn't want to justify avoiding our pain? They would parrot: "we are powerful creators, so we can just imagine we don't have any pain!" This is actually called suppression and avoidance.

This is the perfect strategy for deception, because a soul that is not embodied into the lower chakras are not fully here. They can make no real difference in the material world. They can believe in angels and spirits all they want, but they are of no real danger to the false matrix.

Our multi-dimensional vessel and process of incarnation is intimately and powerfully connected to all of creation. This is the mechanics of being a creator being. Humanity was intentionally designed to have a multidimensional vessel capable of Co-Creation with the fabric of reality. This capacity can only be activated if the soul is property aligned and anchored through the energy body into the physical body.

Unfortunately, if you were born in a hospital, went to public school, watched TV and ate artificial food - your subconscious and somatic body undoubtedly carry trauma from multidimensional abused. This abuse occurs at the fundamental, creational levels of our existence. Meaning that the pain and agony of confusion and separation from our own divine source is both tremendous and difficult to pinpoint if we are not looking for it intently.

This pain severely disrupts our capacity to wield our power as creator beings, and only through releasing, restoring, processing and integrating these suffering parts of our self can we truly move into our sovereign creatorship. By accepting and gaining the space and presence to hold space for the shadow, we become invincible, omnipotent and incredibly loving beings of divine creation. We begin to remember the truth of our own Angelic beingness.

The inherent state of light (consciousness) which penetrates all unified aliveness is that of love, joy, beauty, peace and celebration. All of nature exists in this bountiful frequency of life. A part of nature we are also made up of this same energy of liveliness - our original state.

We are meant to live and exist and create inside that frequency of what might be called Angelic Consciousness. In truth, all consciousness was originally angelic - this is the way my Soul is guided to use and restore the coding of this word. Angelic consciousness can be felt in nature, pulsing through every strand of life. expansive, joyful, confident, serene, connected, mystical, curious, alive, loving, peaceful…

We are returning to this state. In misunderstanding of polarity, some dub these sensations "positive" and "polarized" and I would say this is not true. I would say that a fallen state of consciousness is more like an illness than the opposite of angelic. Just like a healthy ripe apple is not the opposite as a rotten one. And being sick with cancer is not the opposite of simply existing as one is meant to, in perfect health.

Loving and the lack of love are not on the same spectrum of the same thing. Not love is just the absence of love - while love exists in an infinite spectrum of itself. This simple misappropriation of polarity might be a clever fib, an excuse to prolong and allow senseless suffering. These clever spiritual lies such as polarity are deep subconscious reversal codes which keep us from remembering our true origins and heaven as it was intended for us.

Certain deep conditioning and programming forces us to accept fallen states of pain, separation and sexual misery as normal. They force us to become more passionate about our suffering than our grace.

I learn a lot by sitting in the forest, where Nature reigns. Nature is one and the same pulsing through all of life, which includes our own soul. The Nature of Life is also our Human Nature. When I sit to watch the wild life, the trees and soil and water, I see a mirror reflection of Angelic Consciousness. There are no wars and no possession. No rage and no seeking pleasure in another's pain and suffering.

This all tells me that the degradation of consciousness is a virus pervasive in humanity only (but that's not to say that our degraded vibration of consciousness did not affect the natural world) and invites me to explore this further to understand why this has happened, who's agenda this serves, and how we can restore our Divinity and create a better world for All of Life on Earth.

Lucidity Medicine for the Great Sickness

This is sort of a lead-into our next book and multi-media project "Advanced Lightwork: Medicine for the Great Sickness." This will be a self-healing and activation manual, which will be released with 40+ full length recordings of shamanic healings and oracle transmissions designed to assist anyone through a full system reprogramming, and reconnection with the organic living creation.

I share with an integrated presence of neutrality, Divinity, Love and Sovereignty, of distortions which still exist in our world and bodies which require our aligned, empowered right action. It is the solutions and antidotes for deep multidimensional personal and planetary healing and empowerment. It is fuel for timeline acceleration. It is a summary of my findings on Earth through the perspective of a galactic anthropologist and geneticist.

I hope that through this transmission, we can truly anchor our own grace, compassion, love and devotion into our whole body - and discover our own unique expression of those things which are medicines that heal and restore our world to the Heaven we intended.

~ ✣ ~

The relationship between astral implantation and trauma are interdependent, comparable to the saying "which came first, the chicken or the egg." Let's take a deeper look at these multidimensional imbalances by viewing the reflections in our external 3D reality.

Drastic levels of mental illness appearing in citizens of all ages, mass extinction of living beings, dramatic amounts of environmental pollution and degradation. It is not a conspiracy or rocket science to recognize that something is extremely off kelter.

To become Lucid in our living dream, we must become keenly aware of our inner and outer landscapes. This process of awakening includes remembering the truth of our spiritual and divine aspects, but unfortunately many new agers get stuck here. This remembrance of our innate divinity is only the very first step, as with this maturity, we awaken to the grim realities we have come to restore.

We did not come here to "ascend" into our "rainbow bodies" to disappear from the darkness of this world, nor to aboard spaceships that would take us to a distant heavenly world. We came to bring our light and wisdom to this physical world, to revive its lively ancient heavenly magic.

Playing the character of Galactic Anthropologist, I devoted my life in these 7 years of training to seeing lucidly with my own eyes through awakening my energy body and psychic perception. Accessing the different skills and knowledge of higher aspects of my own soul granted me different dimensional perspectives on this reality, and I have finally come to a shareable complete observation.

There is an inter-dimensional force which had a deep and effective agenda to enslave and control humanity, and siphon our energy. There are inter-dimensional systems of energy harvesting, which can be perceived similarly as technology. These systems exist in a higher density than 3D, imperceptible to the common senses.

The energies which are most delectable to the entities which created these harvesting technologies are those of fear, pain, heart-break and sexual misery. As these entities have severed their own connection to source and are no longer nurtured or sustained by love, they can only continue life through the harvesting of degraded energy which move towards death.

The moment we are in on Earth right now is one of massive cleaning. Yes, the big boss of the reversal energy harvesting operation has been removed, so in fact there is no war to fight. In that sense, we have already won.

However that does not mean we are finished with our work here, not even close. I would say that this is again the beginning of our work, since as you can see with your own physical eyes, the majority of humanity are still bound by unconscious programming, trauma and separation. It's as if the war is finished, but the forest is now a barren wasteland covered in blood and corpses - and it will take time to heal, clean and restore.

Angelic Consciousness

In closing of this book, I want to speak these final words on Angelic Consciousness. Angelic Consciousness is the Original State of Consciousness energy which penetrates through all realities and animates all of Life. It is experienced as free flowing, joyful, peaceful, curious, in wonder, loving, trusting and creative. This is our Natural, Originally Intended State of Being.

We recognize that humanity has fallen from this state of pure existence, now carrying thousands of years of distortion and pain, trauma and degradation. None of that however devoids us any Worthiness of the Truth of our Self and our inherent Divinity.

For a long time, multidimensional captors enslaved humanity by creating these bars of self loathing, unworthiness and degradation. These were the very viruses used against humanity making it possible to enslave us. In a lot of ways, our ownership and addiction to our pain is a stockholm syndrome keeping us enslaved inside our own self.

These viruses made us feel we are not worthy of love, or abundance, or life itself without sacrificing vital aspects of our self. These viruses are propagated across generations through mass trauma based mind control until it is so pervasive that it is commonly accepted as normal.

In the end, everything moves us back into our Own Empowerment. If we are held captive by our own beliefs, traumas and distortions, we can simply Heal our Self to re-align and remember the Truth of our Divine Origins and set ourself Free.

How would our lives look like if we could exist in a perpetual state of peace, love, creativity and joy? Are there parts of us that believe this is not possible, and that suffering is simply a facet of life?

I'm looking forward to sharing the Medicines made available through these frequencies of Angelic Consciousness and Original DNA, in Advanced Lightwork: Medicine for the Great Sickness.

I Pray that the Truth of Divine Love penetrates every dimension and time-space, to set every captive aspect free. For all parts of the Oneness to Remember and Experience our innate and inherent Birth Right which is our Love. I pray that all beings are liberated into the remembrance and experiencing of this Love - and that we may together co-create a heavenly existence for all future generations to come.